The
Challenge of
Human Diversity

Third Edition

The Challenge of Human Diversity

Mirrors, Bridges, and Chasms

Third Edition

DeWight R. Middleton

State University of New York College, Oswego

For information about this book, contact:
Waveland Press, Inc.
4180 IL Route 83, Suite 101
Long Grove, IL 60047-9580
(847) 634-0081
info@waveland.com
www.waveland.com

Contents

v

Preface and Acknowledgments

In deciding what changes to make in this new edition, I strove to maintain the core integrity of the previous editions—the message that in order to understand others better, we need to see both similarities and differences among cultures to discover their meaning for us and for them. The chapter on comparative thought remains as a critical ingredient in developing an expanded view of humankind. New in this edition are sections on applied anthropology in chapters 3, 4, and 5. The increasing numbers of anthropologists working in the applied realm compel us to consider some of the pitfalls and ethical dilemmas they face. They face not only the daunting challenges inherent in fieldwork but also additional ones often related to the organization they work for and the goals they hope to reach. To help others is a worthy motivation, but it can be marred by unintended consequences. I have streamlined the discussion of Tylor and Morgan's contributions to anthropology in chapter 5. The remainder of the book remains much the same, except for changes for accuracy, continuity, and flow. I continue to benefit from the support of Peg, Leida, and Chandra. Thanks again to Jeni Ogilvie for her superb work and to Tom Curtin for his continuing support. I am alone responsible for whatever shortcomings this book might have.

The Challenge
of Diversity

The police beat a black man in Los Angeles, provoking a national discussion of race and police brutality, and later sparking a riot in South Central Los Angeles. American public opinion rises against illegal Mexican and Haitian immigrants. Gays fight for equality in the American military, and for the right to marry. In Germany, skinheads terrorize foreign workers. The Soviet empire collapses and Yugoslavia disintegrates into ethnic hatred and killing as Croats, Serbs, and Muslims strike out against each other. Iraqis gas Kurds in northern Iraq, while Hutus and Tutsis slaughter each other in Burundi. The French-speaking Province of Quebec attempts to secede from Canada. Native peoples of the world's rain forests suffer ecological, cultural, and personal assaults from outsiders in the name of progress. Foreign terrorists bring down the twin towers of the World Trade Center in New York City and force a plane to smash into the Pentagon in Washington, D.C.

Problems arising from human diversity are widespread, persistent, and often intractable; they challenge severely our ability to cope with differences on intellectual and practical levels. In part, our problems in coping with issues of human diversity stem from simple misinformation, misunderstanding, and ignorant speculation about the meaning of physical and cultural differences. In part, they spring from a history of suspicion and cycles of violence and revenge between groups that sustain antagonistic relationships and impede rapprochement between them. Ignorance and troubled histories are churned by political and economic competition that further muddies our thinking about matters of diversity. Learning how to unravel the tangled complexities that often prevail in group relationships will take us a long

1

way toward grasping the critical variables operating in specific cases of trouble.

We cannot escape issues of diversity; they are all around us. Travel abroad will increase as the tempo of international business transactions and tourism accelerates (Chambers 2010). College students are entering study abroad programs in growing numbers. The world is increasingly interconnected electronically with voice, image, and text communication, raising international questions of standards, access, and control. Will these increased cultural contacts present new arenas for culture wars or for further cultural homogenization?

Staying at home certainly will not insulate us from problems; barely a handful of culturally homogeneous nations exist today (Nielsson 1985). If anything, comprehending diversity at home may be even more difficult because it is more immediate, threatening, and inescapable. Social distance need not be matched by great geographical distance to cause mischief. There is sufficient diversity within individual societies to distort communication. For example, Deborah Tannen's (1990) work shows how males and females of the same culture, using the same language, talk past each other. They do so because gender differences shape their experience in the larger cultural world in dissimilar ways. Consequently, the same words can take on different meanings according to gender. In addition to gender, divergence of experience may be fostered by variables of age, social class, religious membership, urban or rural location, ethnicity, geographical region, or occupation, to mention a few. Performing different jobs within an organization of any kind can produce small or large worlds of difference that sometimes seem almost insurmountable.

People are often more inclined to be tolerant, perhaps unaccompanied by understanding, of other ways of life outside their own culture, but less so of subcultural differences in their own. Geographical distance somehow seems to make it safer to be understanding, while at the same time you can better ignore whatever they do that you don't like. We might even think that people in our culture ought to know better, and we give them less room for difference. Nonetheless, the same principles for understanding cultural difference apply just as much to intracultural difference as to intercultural difference.

We are faced, then, with the pressing need to develop the art of living together by striking a balance between our differences and similarities. Cultural chasms develop out of our differences, real or imagined, but we can build bridges across these divides based on our similarities. We can do so, however, only if we are willing, by observing others, to look at ourselves in a cultural mirror and thereby see ourselves in a fresh light. This means that we all need to learn to understand others and ourselves and to identify the critical historical and competitive contexts in which we conduct our dialogue with each other.

UNDERSTANDING DIVERSITY

In this text, we focus on *human diversity,* not the politically charged term, "multiculturalism." By human diversity, we mean both biological and physical variations and their significance in various natural and social environments around the world. The problems of human diversity are complex, widespread, and continuing. The purpose of this book is to meet the challenge of human diversity by supplying the necessary information, concepts, and perspectives to grasp the dynamics of human interaction at both group and personal levels. At its conclusion, readers will be better able to think analytically and critically about differences and similarities among human groups, to appreciate personally the risks and the rewards of engaging others, and to understand the necessity for making the effort in the first place.

Acquiring a framework of understanding and making a genuine effort to address issues will permit us to establish the solid base we need to understand how deep cultural differences are formed and maintained. Further, the lessons learned in this effort also can be applied to gender and class differences, as well as differences arising out of disease and disabilities. They apply even to various units within complex organizations, for example, differences among college students, faculty, administration, and support staff. Wherever differences are generated and become impediments to establishing common ground, these lessons will apply. This is not just an agenda for a dominant majority to understand victimized minorities, but for all groups to understand each other and themselves.

Of what practical use is this understanding we hope to gain by the application of our framework? We hope, of course, to better inform our policies and practices regarding other groups, but is there a more direct, practical way of doing this? Anthropologists have become more interested in doing so, and thus the growing subfield of applied anthropology. We will refer to the work of applied anthropologists occasionally as we develop our framework.

THE STRATEGY OF ANTHROPOLOGY

Cultural anthropology's strategy to comprehend other ways of life entails: (1) *direct contact,* (2) *extended contact,* and (3) a *comparative perspective.* The principle of direct contact compels one to live with others on their own turf, generally under their conditions. No armchair philosophizing, or imaginative discussions over cocktails, or sharing of mutual ignorance, stereotypes, or preconceptions will do. Whether you are observing people in a jungle, a central city ghetto, or a middle-class suburb, you must go where they are and not speculate about them from afar.

Extended contact means that you can't just drop in for a day or two, give a questionnaire, and leave. It means you spend quality research time and participate in daily life as much as permitted. It means months and years of effort depending on the nature of the research and real-life contingencies. If necessary, you must learn another language. Then you must attempt to place that particular experience and understanding in a larger, comparative context that enhances our general understanding of the human condition in both its universal and local expressions. The comparative perspective helps us to understand specific cultures, and specific cultures contribute to our knowledge of many cultures—in a feedback loop between the general and the specific.

Increasingly, the successful field project is seen as a *dialogue* between informant and anthropologist, an exchange between two cultures. Anthropologists are known as those who study other cultures, but in fact anthropologists are forced by the nature of fieldwork to study their own, too. Conceiving fieldwork as dialogue recognizes the fact that observers bring to the field their own culture, and that their arrival affects the very community that they observe. Observer and observed are observing each other and each is trying to make sense of the other in terms of her own culture. Anthropologists, for example, may ask scores of questions, some of which have never before been asked in that culture. Thus, the insiders also learn something of their own culture even if only to reaffirm it in the face of probing questions asked by an outsider. Paul Rabinow (1977:116–121) reports an example from Morocco. He and an informant, Malik, were working on a profile of the socioeconomic variations in the village. Rabinow suggested they examine Malik's socioeconomic status, but as they did so Malik became uncomfortable.

> The "facts" which were emerging did not correspond to his cultural categories. Moroccan villagers are not in the habit of totaling up their parcels of land, calculating their combined holdings, comparing them with the rising and falling prices of goods, and making systematic and quantitative comparisons with their neighbors. Nor did they understand their village conceptually in terms of socioeconomic strata. . . .
>
> Malik began to see that there was a disparity between his self-image and my classification system. (Rabinow 1977:117–118)

For Malik, the local culture dictated that things were either going well or not going well. That was the only concern the people had. The ethnographer's questions, and conceptual reorganization of the village in outsider terms, made Malik reflect on his own circumstances from a new perspective. He was challenged, and it made him uncomfortable.

Because Rabinow reflected on his informant's response to his question, rather than just fixing on the hard facts it yielded, he was able to reach a new level of understanding.

Similarly, ethnographer Michael Jackson, an advocate of radical empiricism, which underscores the importance of participating in events rather than just passively recording them, states:

> The importance of this view for anthropology is that it stresses the ethnographer's *interactions* with those he or she lives with and studies, while urging us to clarify the ways in which our knowledge is grounded in our practical, personal, and participatory experience in the field as much as our detached observations. Unlike traditional empiricism which draws a definite boundary between observer and observed, between method and object, radical empiricism denies the validity of such cuts and makes the *interplay* between these domains the focus of interest. (1989:3)

Taking notes without real participation maintains distance between the observed and the observer. Living in a culture is better than not being there, but living in a culture and dispassionately taking notes is a limited form of participation. The dialogue of fieldwork is not just about talking, but participating wherever possible and prudent. No one can say precisely what the proper mix of participation and observation is, because the answer depends on a number of variables including the nature of the study, the personality of the observer, and the local situation. No anthropologist would take the extreme position in either case but would recognize to varying degrees that a mix of approaches yields the richest harvest.

Good rapport with one's informants rests on a respect for the other's way of life, even outlandish and repugnant ways. Paul Stoller (1989:156) observes that a "deep respect for other worlds and other ideas, ideas often preposterous to our way of thinking, is central to the ethnographic endeavor." Respect awards value to a people's imperfect struggle with life, a struggle that binds us all in common cause. Respect for other ways entails certain ethical standards of behavior, not the least of which is the protection of informant confidentiality and anonymity and the reasonable security of collected data. Anthropologists work with *informants,* not informers. These terms are sometimes confused with each other, but they do not have the same meaning: informers "rat" or "squeal" on others engaged in illegal conduct (although anthropologists sometimes study illegal behavior); informants instruct us in the various aspects of their accepted way of life. Anthropologists are normally exceedingly careful about how they conduct themselves in the field as a matter of ethics and for the obvious reason that they depend on the cooperation of the insiders to learn about their culture. The American Anthropological Association, as well as its sister organizations, has a Code of Ethics to guide such work.

Anthropologists have discovered historically that the road to understanding other cultures is littered with hazards for which there are few warning signs. The road has taken us much longer to travel and the destination of objective knowledge has been more elusive than we first thought it would be. The ethnocentric view that one's own way of life is the best, the most natural and right, always lurks in our unconscious mind and is often challenged only by the contradictions we observe in another culture. Because of the biases of amateur anthropologists in the 1800s, early professional anthropologists invented the idea of *cultural relativism* to guard against the natural tendency of humans to prejudge other cultures and to drag our own cultural baggage to the field with us. Cultural relativism advocates understanding other ways of life in their contexts. Anthropologists try to find out what *is,* not what should be from our point of view. We pursue the goal of withholding judgment and striving for an accurate understanding of a culture on its own terms. Melville Herskovits (1973), who wrote a great deal about cultural relativism, observed that this precept calls for a "tough minded" attitude to try to understand the Other's point of view, however repugnant it is to us, without allowing our own to distort our observations and conclusions about him. This ideal may be almost impossible to achieve completely in reality, but the ideal is one that we need to strive for, nevertheless.

Unfortunately, the public often misunderstands cultural relativism to advocate amorality and behavioral anarchy. Anthropologists probably have allowed the public to think so by not doing a better job of explaining the precept. By insisting that a culture should be understood in terms of its own logic, anthropologists seem to be saying that anything goes, there are no universal standards of behavior, and thus, we leave open the door to public misunderstanding. But the historical intention of anthropologists like Herskovits was, like the early professionals, to focus on the task of doing objective fieldwork in order to give anthropology a solid database and thus distinguish it from the amateur work of the 1800s. Anthropologists know full well that human societies cannot survive in the face of behavioral anarchy and amorality. Advocating such would be to encourage our own demise. Culture, including moral principles, guides human behavior so that we work sufficiently well together to survive in groups.

Anthropologists do not condone various forms of behavior simply because they observe them in the field. To report them is not to advocate them. Cultural relativism is in this sense a methodological point of view, not a moral stance. It is not just other cultures, of course, that we need to be tough-minded about, but also our own so that we will understand our own biases. Furthermore, people in other cultures will have prejudged us also. This is why good fieldwork includes productive dialogues, the give-and-take of participant observation, between the observed and the observer.

This book does not assume that the reader is or wants to be an anthropologist. It does advance the idea that the lessons anthropologists offer are time-tested and fire-hardened and that they can enhance the nonprofessional's grasp of human diversity. The methods, while not perfect, are based on those important principles that often work to improve everyday human relationships. Even without anthropological expertise we can make a serious, extended, and informed effort to tap into the experience of others and to see the world from their point of view. Doing so does not mean that we agree with their point of view, or behavior—of course, they have the same options about us. The result of enlightened effort is likely to be an informed and reflective engagement leading to better communication.

Offered as the core of this book is the following argument: all humans are essentially the same and share the same basic capacity for thinking and feeling as well as for social and moral reasoning (Brown 1991). This general capacity takes specific cultural shape as particular groups of humans endeavor to survive in different environments and historical situations. A critically important part of human efforts to fashion a living in the desert, in the jungle, or in the city, adjacent to other humans, is to construct over time *a cultural tradition, a continuing set of shared customs, knowledge, and beliefs, that helps humans to reach their goals . . . a blueprint for living.*

Because each of us is emotionally and habitually committed to a tradition, we find it difficult to break its bounds. But we can, with earnest and informed effort, weaken our tradition's constraints sufficiently to come to know a different way of life. Individuals have done so for millennia. The secret in accomplishing this task lies in mapping the problems, interests, and experiences of people from their point of view, while striving to control the bias of our own tradition. Toward this end, we will build a framework of analysis that handles the fact that all cultures bear both similarities and differences and explains why it is often so hard for people to communicate across cultural borders (Brown 1991, Hall 1990).

PLAN OF THE BOOK

We confront directly the challenge of visiting other cultures in chapter 1, "Culture Shock," where we explore the process of fitting into another culture and give particular attention to understanding what various cross-cultural incidents tell us about this uncertain process.

In chapter 2, "Our Common Ground," we define our commonality rather than our differences. We trace our origins, examine our senses, understand how we structure experience, and establish some universal characteristics of human culture. Chapter 3, "Our Lived Difference," describes how we become different through our lived experience—how this experience of time and place contributes to what we do, what we believe, and what we value. We note also the approach of applied anthropology in negotiating differences in order to develop successful improvement projects.

In chapter 4, "Mirrors and Chasms," we let others speak to us about their experiences in contact with us, and we re-examine as well our own progress in revealing our ethnocentrism (judging another culture by the standards of our own). We discuss the resurgence of minority groups around the world, and the ethics of fieldwork in applied projects. In chapter 5, "The Comparative Perspective," we establish the importance and inevitability in anthropology of comparative thinking, trace briefly some of the past mistakes in the use of the comparative perspective, develop an overview of the evolution of increasingly complex societies, and apply the comparative perspective to McDonald's restaurants international operation. We close with a note on how the comparative perspective helps practicing anthropologists to establish a body of best practices. In chapter 6, "Meeting the Challenge of Global Issues," we extend our discussion of McDonald's as an example of globalization and as a symbol of Western—especially U.S.—success. We finish by raising some questions about the future.

Chapter One

Culture Shock

The English were quite right. One had to dress for dinner. One needed a symbol, some external sign, to assist daily remembrance of what one was. It did not occur to me that the need for such artificial aids was alien to me and a sign that I was no longer myself. Instead, to help me over the next seven weeks, I called the cook and gave detailed orders for a Thanksgiving dinner. At the same time I told Sunday to lay out evening clothes, set the table with my best, and put out all the liquor in a fine array. I was no longer trying to learn how to survive in my new environment; I was concerned with sealing myself off from it. (Bowen [1954] 1964:238–239)

When we visit another country we customarily complain about a variety of problems. We find the place too hot, too cold, too wet, or too dry. We encounter foods that sicken us, odors that nauseate us, and sights that startle us. We worry about standards of sanitation and chafe at the lack of bathroom facilities. The "locals" act in strange ways for reasons we cannot fathom. Small children mill about us speaking with ease a language that eludes our adult comprehension. We are treated as curiosities. An alien way of life challenges our most cherished beliefs about who we are, who they are, and the nature of the world in which we both live.

Burdened by these new challenges to our familiar way of life we might respond in anger, depression, or paranoia. Longing for the familiar, we might seek others like ourselves, and search for accustomed food. Withdrawing to the security of our rooms, we might lose ourselves in escapist novels and daydreams of the home we know so well. We might, as Bowen (the nom de plume of Laura Bohannan) notes about her efforts to adjust to fieldwork in Africa, attempt to seal ourselves off for a time from the alien culture, and to recover the familiar.

These responses are symptoms of culture shock. *Culture shock is defined as individual maladaptive behavior emerging under the stress of coping with a foreign way of life.* It is quite natural to feel fatigue and confusion and to seek periods of rest when living in another culture, but when occasional struggle advances to more persistent feelings of hostility and irritability, culture shock has seized us. We become frustrated because we cannot figure out what is going on, or why. These are the rough bumps that threaten to throw us off the road to personal adjustment to a new culture. Culture shock is a painful personal revelation of the profound extent to which we are emotionally and intellectually bound by our experience of growing up in a particular culture. It is also a striking reminder of how exceedingly difficult it can be for us to change our habitual way of life. It is a dramatic example of a human paradox: on the one hand, our success as a species is utterly dependent on our ability to find novel solutions to vexing problems, while, on the other hand, it is novelty that we so often seek to avoid. This curious blend of commitment to both tradition and change, as individuals or in groups, is a paradox rooted in our fundamental nature, as we shall see in the following chapter.

Neither Americans nor the English are unique in complaining about the shocks of life in a strange land. All humans in such circumstances experience similar problems and complain about them too. While these challenges are real, we risk an imbalanced view if we do not at the same time note that many people do come to value their experiences in other worlds with other people; they have stimulating and relatively painless experiences. Nevertheless, we learn much by meeting head-on the widespread problems inherent in adjusting to and understanding other lifeways based on different principles. By confronting these issues we learn more about ourselves as well as others, because culture contact necessarily involves two cultures.

In the remainder of this chapter we shall examine some common experiences of culture shock reported by anthropologists. We use these shocks to help us to understand the personal side of experience in another culture. In the course of this examination, we discover some of the common challenges the outsider faces and develop a preliminary appreciation of the hold that culture has on each of us.

SHOCKS TO THE SYSTEM

The situations in which people find themselves as they grapple initially with cultural differences range from the humorous and merely embarrassing to the dangerous and emotionally devastating. Barbara Anderson (1990) tells a number of amusing stories of her misadventures in the field, including a hilarious description of being completely flustered in a bath house because of her ignorance of local customs. Napoleon Chagnon (1992) arrived at a village in the Amazon Basin to be greeted by Yanomamo warriors with spears poised menacingly, their faces smeared with green nasal discharge as a result of taking hallucinogenic drugs. Jean Briggs (1970) spent time with a small group of Inuit (Eskimo) feeling very much out of place and exhibiting a generous measure of emotional volatility, which is not the Inuit way. Her inability to conceal her emotions threatened to disrupt their small group harmony. Although most people will not encounter these extremes in their travels, such examples serve to underscore in dramatic ways some of the issues we will tackle in this text.

Challenges to the Senses

Each cultural place is characterized by a distinct profile of sensory experiences that can please or irritate the senses of a visitor. As Barbara Anderson puts it:

> Unlike our overeager brains, our senses remained resistant and disbelieving in the face of Taarnby's new reality. They clung persistently to a learned logic about the proper sources of bodily comfort. We were never oblivious to the smell of the sea. . . . Unprepared taste buds programmed for different foods, scorned all efforts—mine especially—to adapt to the enjoyment of eel or beer soup. Even my nose resisted odors that, I was later to understand, distinguish villages everywhere and become as encoded and subliminally distinctive of a particular community as a DNA profile of a person. (1990:35)

Writing of her stay in Botswana (in Southeastern Africa), Marianne Alverson notes:

> There is a certain strong, acrid smell impossible to ignore. It is by far the worst odor around here; body odor. I think it is caused by sweating into dirty clothes which absorb the smoke of the evening fire. Nevertheless, we sit close together and pass the kadi (beer); and in the process, we have managed to get used to the smell of poverty. (1987:21)

Alverson's case supports the view that North Americans generally are uncomfortable with body odor and tend to associate it with weakness of moral character and personal slovenliness. Alverson, of course, does not make this association. In an environment of tropical heat and persistent drought, the Tswana have little choice. Human and animal consumption of water warrant priority over human bathing. We are accustomed to an extravagant use of water, but taking baths or showers each day as most North Americans do habitually would be an unthinkable waste in such a dry region. Wearing clothes, a cultural value introduced by Westerners accustomed to a temperate climate, is of questionable value in the tropical environment of the Tswana. Often, one of the first acts of Western domination was to put clothing on native people. Wearing clothing raises costly problems of maintenance and replacement that were not a part of native adaptation to the area. These examples suggest that the term "cultural place" is a good descriptive term, because the characteristic odors emanate from the interaction of culture and nature, both physically and conceptually, in the local place.

In another incident, the Alversons were uncomfortable with the large swarms of flies that hovered constantly about them and their compound in certain seasons of the year. Their host replied to their complaint:

> "Certainly there are many flies! Flies mean cattle. If there are many flies in the Lolwapa [compound], a man is said to be rich with cattle. It is no good to destroy flies, or harm will come to the herd. When the herd moves on, so too will the flies." (Alverson 1987:390)

We associate flies with dirt and disease, while the Tswana consider them to be a desirable sign of wealth, because they are mainly cattle herders. North Americans certainly are not unfamiliar with flies, but the unrelenting swarms that engulfed the Alversons were a nuisance, partly because Americans tend to associate them with disease and negatively value them. We take for granted our interpretations of what we sense until challenged by contrary interpretations.

Most new sensory experiences become absorbed quickly into a new routine, although some may remain as lingering irritants. In part, this adjustment follows desensitization through sheer repetition; in part, it emerges from our eventual *classification of sensory data* into an ordered and anticipated world. Initially, the Alversons reacted automatically to the flies as if they were at home. Although their informant's explanation that flies indirectly indicate wealth might not have changed their basic attitude much, it gave them another perspective to think about. Intellectually, they understood that their reaction was relevant to their home experience, not that of the Tswana. It was a start. The clouds of flies were thus made a part of the ordered Tswana world that the Alversons sought to enter.

If some of our new sensory experiences challenge us, still others completely escape our perception.

> "The Basarwa will see here that it is your heel in the sand, that it is the heel of the woman who is not bearing a child, but she is still young. The woman walked slowly when the sun was there," he pointed at the sky and continued. "The woman walked on a day with very little wind, a day with no rain clouds nearby. She walked from the southwest to the southeast and stopped here for something. She walked past the twig broken by the foot of one in man's shoes who was moving east to west when the sun was higher in the

sky. This is the beetle to collect and make poisons for the hunting arrow. The woman who walked here was not a woman of the thirst-land because she had her own food and water. Why would she leave behind a good eating root with water?"

"A good eating root? Where?"

"This here!"

"This?" I pointed to the skimpy vine at the edge of the circle.

"Certainly! It is not enough to see what is on the top of the sand. You must know what is underneath." (Alverson 1987:111–112)

Alverson could neither observe the signs nor read their meaning had she seen them, because she had no experience in doing such things. She could learn this craft from her hosts if she wished, but probably not as well as those who had grown up in the area and learned as second nature to read the sands.

Specialists in human perception have long known that we practice *selective perception*, which means we focus on some parts of our environment while ignoring other parts. We humans are not equipped to give equal attention to all the sensory data that bombard us at any one time. What guides our perception for the most part is interest and experience. In short, we focus on what is important to us. Reading spoor in the desert is a survival skill for desert dwellers, but completely useless for city dwellers. When entering another culture we learn what part of their environment they are interested in and why.

Handling initial perceptions is an important part of building the competence and the confidence to move on to other challenges. Anthropologists record their experiences from the first day of their arrival in a new culture and are often surprised, when later they read their daily journal, at how quickly those initial experiences were absorbed into their unconscious routine (Stoller 1989:3–4). Later, we will revisit the meanings people give to their perceptions of taste and sound.

Communicating

Not speaking the local language or speaking it at a beginner's level of competence makes one feel mute, helpless, and dependent. Not having control over language is particularly frustrating to professionals who are accustomed to speaking in their native language at a high level of competence. Having young children with us may add further to our discomfort because they pick up the local language so quickly— they interact easily with other children.

Even with previous language preparation, we are likely to find ourselves hesitant and fumbling, and given to constant rehearsals of what we intend to say. Linguistic disaster lurks always. Barbara Anderson tells of her experience at coffee hour, when, on her departure, she politely told the host how delicious her pastries were, only to learn later that she actually had said to her startled but bemused host that the food was "goddamned good" (1990:98). Martha Ward, having stepped accidentally on a woman's toes during her work on Pohnpei, in the Pacific, apologized by mistakenly blurting out "His canoe is blue" (2005:17). The people we are visiting are likely to appreciate our willingness to learn their language because the effort validates the worth of their language, but the effort may place us on the horns of a dilemma. On the one hand, if we get a few phrases correct people might leap to the unwarranted conclusion that we know more than we do and slip into their normal speed and style of delivery. On the other hand, overconfidence on our part might lead us into further trouble. Moritz Thomsen, a Peace Corps worker, describes the following event.

> Another example of my facility with Spanish: in Ecuador an introduction is a rather formal moment. You are presented to an Ecuadorian, who nicely says that he is absolutely enchanted to meet you and that he is at your service—*a sus ordenes*. For months I simply acknowledged these gracious speeches of pleasure by mumbling over and over, "*mucho gusto Señor, mucho gusto.*" But later, bloated with a self-confidence that had no basis in reality, I began to reply with a few gracious comments of my own, *a su servicio*, I would say smiling brightly and shaking my new friend's hand. "A su servicio," at your service. Someone drew me aside one day and pointed out very discreetly that if I were saying anything at all, I was only offering a toast, "here's to your bathroom," and that in many cases, particularly if the man had no bathroom, I might conceivably be treading on some sensitive nerve endings. (1969:62)

Not only is this a fine case of "bloated self-confidence," but also a good example of the need to acquire a second level of competence in the *social connotations* of the words we learn to speak.

Laura Bohannan writes of the confusion between her and her informants:

> It was Accident who made me see the difficulty. As he talked, I again realized that learning the language and learning the culture were mutually dependent. I had misunderstood because I did not know the full social implications of the words. ([1954] 1964:110)

> They did not grasp the nature of my difficulty. Like everyone else, they assumed that if I used a word at all, I must be fully aware of all that it implied. ([1954] 1964:111)

Developing sensitivity to speech behavior in varying social contexts is often important. Ward (2005:59), for example, had to deal with "honorific" and routine levels of speaking. That is, she had to learn to speak one way to the titled social elite and another to communicate with commoners on a daily basis. Most cultures are socially differentiated in various ways, and language nuances are often geared to these differences. Language performance, then, is sensitive to social and situational contexts in ways that may not be immediately apparent to the outsider.

The sharpened attention we give to speaking and translating in an unfamiliar language is tiring. Add to this essential task the constant pressure of being on stage and subject to critical scrutiny, and one can easily understand how entering another culture can be a fatiguing, albeit rewarding, experience.

Interpreting body language can be an equally treacherous adventure because much of it is not universal, but culture bound. In North America, beckoning someone is accomplished by waving someone to you with elbow down, hand up, palm toward you, and the hand moved as if pulling the person to you. In Ecuador, it is customary to put palm down, elbow to side, and wave as if signaling, from our point of view, someone to go away. Thus, situations arise where an Ecuadorian is verbally telling you to "come here," while simultaneously motioning you "to go away." The visitor is apt to stand frozen to the spot while the Ecuadorian intensifies her attempt to get you to come to her.

Elizabeth Hahn gives an example of misreading body language in Tonga, an island of the Pacific. Visiting a Tongan bureaucrat early in her fieldwork:

> I was having my first "anthropological" discussion—one profession-
> al to another. And then it happened—in the middle of one of my ex-
> planations, he started raising and wiggling his eyebrows at me. I
> was taken completely off guard and stammered to a stop. He
> stopped. No sooner had I resumed talking than he started giving
> me the eye again. We started and stopped several times. I began to
> get very angry. There he was looking so innocent with a quizzical
> expression on his face, as if I were the one doing something odd.
> How dare he come on to me? (1990:73)

Completely baffled by wiggling eyebrows, Hahn compounds the problem by attributing to the bureaucrat, also puzzled at the halting flow of conversation, a motive understandable in our culture. She assumes that he has made a fully conscious decision to act in a particular manner, when he is actually performing habitual, and therefore mostly unconscious, behavior. He has no idea why she is acting so peculiarly. She learns later that such eyebrow action is the Tongan equivalent of "uh huh," or "I hear you"—in other words, a conversational lubricant.

Martha Ward (2005) also learned quickly that on Pohnpei a high-status person should not touch the head of a child because the head of a lower-status person is vulnerable to a flow of power from the higher status person, resulting in sickness. A variation in this belief is found throughout Latin America where it is thought that if a higher status person stares directly at a child he can induce sickness in the child.

Social Use of Food

Choices of food are both personal and cultural and frequently difficult to change, because we become so accustomed to a particular diet. In general, North Americans are not organ eaters. Inuit eat raw seal, but even North American consumers of rare steak want it cooked some. Native peoples find a good source of protein in insects and grubs. In the Orient, cats and dogs are fair game, while for us they are household pets. Some peoples eat eel or snakes. The cattle herders of East Africa drink raw milk mixed with blood drawn from their cattle. The banana-like plantain, to North Americans quite bland with the consistency of cork when heated, is the valued bread of much of South America. Others would find some of our food equally repugnant.

In areas of scarce resources, eating the entire animal is a matter of survival, and good social taste. Eating the entire beast as a matter of survival doesn't mean that people do not also enjoy it. They will eat all they can in one sitting. Only by living with such people can we appreciate their motivation to consume all they can when they have the chance.

> Both of us ate ravenously, ignoring the children who gathered to watch the performance. I could feel my stomach distending as I forced more and more food into it. It was a habit we had learned since our arrival. When there is food, eat as much as you can. You never know when you will eat again. A couple of lean days had persuaded us of the truth of this unspoken aphorism. Today we had the sensation which the Sherente cherish and which is much celebrated in their stories: the pleasure of feeling our bellies grow big with food. (Maybury-Lewis [1965] 1988:52)

Not to eat the entire animal would seem to the Sherente a ridiculous waste of food. After all, they had no way of storing it nor any knowledge of when they would kill another animal. Even if we come to eat the local food routinely, we still, at times, might be driven to search for ice cream in Ecuador, a fast-food outlet in Cairo, Chinese cuisine in Nairobi, or pizza in Jakarta.

Anthropologists are known to take certain treasured foods, such as peanut butter, into the field with them where they hoard them. By these efforts, we attempt to recover the familiar and comfortable, to seal ourselves off as Laura Bohannan comments in the beginning of this chapter, however momentarily, from the other culture. Note what Janet Siskind says about her experience:

> At times when I found life at Marcos frustrating and lonely, I revenged myself childishly by eating crackers and jam in my *mosquitero* [mosquito netting hung over a bed], opening the large can as quietly as possible since children can hear a cracker can opening over an incredible distance. Despite my caution someone would come by and ask what I was doing. I would reply that I was reading,

though no one believed me. Giving and receiving food are important emotion-laden interactions at Marcos. Eating with people is an affirmation of kinship. Refusing to share food is a denial of all relationships, a statement that the other is an outsider. When people are eating and offer nothing, one feels more than hunger, one feels alien and alienated. (1973:9)

In Siskind's situation, to lie is the lesser evil; it is a social fiction shared with her neighbors so that she not be is considered antisocial in their terms. Had she been a relative and they found out that she was hoarding food, there would have been considerable tension if not serious conflict.

Food, as Siskind notes, is a form of social communication. Who eats with whom and under what circumstances is a statement about social relationships. Even those human groups living the simplest technological existence, the San of the Kalahari Desert of South Africa, for example, have rules of food distribution and consumption that are determined mostly by kinship distance from the hunter most responsible for the kill. Such rules express expectations of sharing in routine ways and reduce potential sources of group conflict. They make a statement about community life.

In a quarter of Marrakech, residents tell Elizabeth Fernea that they did not understand why she and her husband were constantly having dinner guests. They could not decide what was going on because Moroccan custom is to have social dinners only at ceremonial times such as weddings and funerals. As one informant put it, "it isn't our custom to have people for dinner just for fun" ([1976] 1988:344). Similarly, when the Ferneas were asked to dinner by Omar, who was better acquainted with Western ways and with Elizabeth's husband, Robert, the neighbors could not understand his purpose. There appeared to be no ceremonial occasion. When the Ferneas arrived at Omar's, they ate alone as is the custom. Only after the meal was finished, hands washed, and tea served, did the host family join them. They seemed caught between two worlds; on the one hand they were invited to Omar's, counter to custom, but were entertained according to local custom for rare, nonceremonial visitors.

Understandings about the distribution and consumption of food are culturally shaped so early in life that they are taken as a natural state of affairs. In the following example, both parties commit the *fallacy of naive realism*, the unconscious assumption that some acts are so basic and simple that they always carry the same meaning across cultures.

There are still patterns of past social interaction which I engage in without thinking. It is only when they are inappropriate that I even become aware of them. Here a host does not question visitors as to their preference. After all there is no choice. If kadi has been brewed, the beer must be offered. If there is no kadi, tea is cooked and served. When serving, a host does not ask visitors whether they

wish a refill, for to a Tswana, such questioning reveals a lack of gen-
erosity and true friendship. (Alverson 1987:52)

Alverson kept asking her visitors, to their chagrin, if they wanted
refills. The increasingly tense atmosphere perplexed her. Beneath this
tension lay those naive and hidden assumptions on both sides that certain acts of hospitality are so fundamental to human nature, they
should be easily understood by everyone. Yet both parties are challenged by puzzling words and facial expressions that indicate something is wrong. In this case, their willingness to discuss the confusion
resulting from this "simple," but culturally defined act of hospitality
helped each party to discover something important about both themselves and the other. Hahn's encounter with the bureaucrat in Tonga,
the one who wiggled his eyebrows, is another example of naive realism.

Customs dedicated to giving or receiving, whether service or food,
present to the unwary outsider another hazard on the road to adjustment. David Counts tells of his experience in Papua New Guinea where
he managed to shame his village host by purchasing watermelon. The
emotionally painful event led him to the following conclusion: "In a
society where food is shared or gifted as part of social life, you may not
buy it with money" ([1990] 2000:178). Later, he was overwhelmed with
gifts of bananas and tried to refuse additional stalks, an act that immediately brought a return visit from his already embarrassed host. This
time his host admonished him by saying that if he had more stalks than
he could eat, he should give some to his visitors. Counts learned a second lesson. "Never refuse a gift, and never fail to return a gift. If you
cannot use it, you can always give it away to someone else—there is no
such thing as too much—there are never too many bananas" ([1990]
2000:181). His final lesson: "where reciprocity is the rule and gifts are
the idiom, you cannot demand a gift, just as you cannot refuse a gift"
([1990] 2000:183). Although not claiming a scholarly conclusion regarding universal rules of reciprocity—these are, in fact, very common ideas
cross-culturally—Counts nevertheless demonstrates his wish to
uncover the cultural principles of giving and receiving necessary to
guide him in his future interactions in New Guinea.

Cultural expectations about giving and receiving are important
because the circumstances of exchange are statements about social
relationships, and to violate the rules of exchange is therefore to violate
the standards of normative social interaction. It is important for an
outsider to acquire an early grasp of these rules.

Gender Roles

Being an outsider has both costs and benefits. When we hear of an
outsider being inducted into a clan or tribe, we tend to think that the
person is being honored. Indeed, outsiders are so honored on occasion.

But it is more likely that the outsider is simply being placed in a familiar role in the local social structure in order to define how local people will interact with her. An outsider role is awkward and confusing because it carries no familiar expectations guiding social interaction. Siskind (1973:15) notes that her work with Sharanahua informants in Peru was difficult and tense because she fit no existing role in their society. Jean-Paul Dumont ([1978] 1992) tried to behave in a manner designed to prevent his Panare hosts from classifying him in various outsider roles. He drank some alcohol, for example, to avoid being classified as a Christian missionary. But, when one of his informants made him a brother, he wondered if he and the Panare meant the same thing by the term. Was he a literal or a figurative brother? The new classification did succeed in giving him somewhat of an insider status and, as a result, improved the Panares' behavior toward him, as well as his toward them. Still, he remained unconvinced that he was a true brother in the Panare sense.

Being an outsider sometimes gives one some freedom of movement not accorded to male and female insiders, and we can sometimes negotiate other allowances as Regina Oboler (1986) managed during her time with the Nandi of Kenya. Being an outsider rarely, however, exempts one completely from the expectations of the host culture. Oboler and her husband had to forget about some of their behavior as an American husband and wife, such as holding hands while walking together in public (1986:39). The woman's role among the Nandi is to walk behind the husband, and Oboler could negotiate no allowance in this case.

In urban settings where people are accustomed to outsiders there is usually more freedom to act and less pressure to "fit in." The limits of familiar roles can be expanded and new roles more easily introduced. The influence of mass media, the rise of a technocrat class, and modernization generally tend to make people more receptive to change; the face-to-face relationship so important to social control in small communities is often missing or softened.

Sometimes, forced changes are subtler. Alverson reports this comment from her husband:

> "I know it's been hard on you," he admitted.
> "We're living on top of each other in this hut, yet we're in separate worlds. Haven't you noticed? We have become a Tswana couple. The men talk to men. The women talk to women. Sometimes they mix, but usually in private, usually in the still of the night." (1987:188)

The Ferneas had a similar experience with social pressures in Morocco. Women are confined to the private domestic realm and the company of other women, while men operate mostly in the public domain among other men. The Ferneas had to adapt.

Both men and women face restrictions on their attempts to gather data from the opposite sex. Segregation of gender role behavior in societies operating under heavy Arab and Islamic cultural influence raises intriguing questions about how a female anthropologist could study effectively any cultural domain other than that of women. Soraya Altorki and Camilla Fawzi El-Sohl (1984) assembled a number of reports from Arab women who worked in Arab culture as PhD anthropologists. The researchers concluded that while there are definite problems, their success depended more on the contingencies of time, place, and the nature of the problem being investigated, than on the inflexibility of gender identity. In general, women have been more successful than men in crossing gender domains for productive study.

There is always a tension between being deeply involved and at the same time trying to escape some of the social constraints imposed by another culture. Anthropologists face the dilemma of being "marginal natives" (Freilich 1968), of trying to be on the inside while knowing that they will always be essentially outsiders. We want it both ways. Jean Briggs (1970) was "made" a daughter, which delighted her until she discovered that she was expected to act like a daughter, and do the work of a daughter. Suddenly, her privileged status was in jeopardy. Laura Bohannan comments on her experience:

> I had longed to be accepted, but I meant something rather different by it: the privilege of going my own way with their full confidence. Udama now pointed out that I could not at the same time claim the guest's privilege of doing more or less as I wished and the family privilege of going behind the scenes. ([1954] 1964:123)

Bohannan elected to go behind the scenes, to participate, but still had trouble with her anthropological conscience to observe, which in turn interfered with her participation. Experienced anthropologists know, as Bohannan did, that productive fieldwork is based on achieving an artful balance between observation and participation. We need to be a part of the community we study, yet free to withdraw when we think we need to for reasons of personal adjustment or maintaining objectivity. Sometimes, anthropologists are caught between rival factions and find it necessary therefore to maintain some distance from issues. Degree and conditions of participation are continuing quandaries of fieldwork.

Age and sex are universal characteristics by which to define role and status obligations, and rights. Learning role and status, perhaps beginning with the family, is a good way of uncovering the expectations and etiquette of social interaction. Outsiders then face Bohannan's question of how much of their own accustomed roles and rights they will give up and how much they will retain. Cultures differ in how lenient they are with those outsiders who do not wish to modify their behavior.

Moral Dilemmas

Living in another culture is an instructive exercise in values clarification. Encountering strange behavior and disparate beliefs will challenge our ideas about what is important in human affairs. We cannot completely avoid these tests even on the tourist circuit, but any serious effort to engage another culture on its own terms is sure to raise many moral issues. Most of these dilemmas will be ultimately irresolvable for the outsider, unless she is prepared to take great risks in advocating change.

Elizabeth Fernea ([1976] 1988:103–104) describes her concern for a man, covered with blood and dirt, lying in the street. She hesitated in the street wondering if she should help and speculating about the extent of his injuries. Why was he lying there unattended with a police station a mere block away? As she stood, trying to read the cultural significance of the scene before her, a man behind her said to her in French "move on"; it was none of her affair. That evening she and her husband, Bob, speculated further on how to read this incident. Was it because she was a foreigner? A woman? Was the injured man drunk? Was his family close by and on their way to aid him? She does not report whether they ever discovered the reason.

Effective action depends on an accurate reading of the situation. When the outsider does not have a clue as to the cultural significance underlying an observed event, she does not know the appropriate action to take. Anthropologists use such mysteries to help them dig deeper into local life ways. But it is critical to remember that it is not just the other culture that is under examination here, but the outsider's as well. Colin Turnbull makes this comparison explicit with respect to the treatment of animals among the Mbuti:

> At other times I have seen Pygmies singeing feathers off birds that were still alive, explaining that the meat is tender if death comes slowly. And the hunting dogs, valuable as they are, get kicked around mercilessly from the day they are born to the day they die. I have never seen any attempt to domesticate any animal or bird apart from the hunting dog. When I talked to the Pygmies about their treatment of animals, they laughed at me and said, "The forest has given us animals for food—should we refuse the gift and starve?" I thought of turkey farms and Thanksgiving, and of the millions of animals reared in our own society with the sole intention of slaughtering them for food. (1962:100)

North Americans have their own dichotomous categories of animals as pets, and animals as food. Our values are shaped on the one hand by romanticized and anthropomorphized stories of animals in our media and, on the other hand, by the fact that we are no longer accustomed to working animals. Some would say that we commit our own form of savagery on experimental laboratory animals for our benefit.

Alverson's (1987) young son began to develop his own ideas about cultural differences, his and the Tswana's, in the treatment of animals.

> "Moremi is—cruel—to the goats. He wouldn't let the limping goat stay in the Kraal. He pushed it out. He made it go on. I tried to stop him. He laughed. He beat it. He kept the baby goat away from its mother. It wanted to drink. He wouldn't let it. Why is he so mean? He never pets them." (p. 25)

> "I know why Moremi doesn't name my goats. People are hungry here. A goat is meat," he said simply. (p. 31)

North Americans do not usually name goats, turkeys, and beef cows either. They also are in the category of food.

North Americans are often angered and frustrated by another culture's poor health conditions that seem simple enough to combat.

> I had very complicated feelings about this child. My relationship with the family was strained on her account. At mealtime, with the baby sleeping on the floor or eating pieces of bananas or rice off the floor, I would get so mad, and so mad at my anger and my inability to function, that I couldn't speak. We had had many discussions about the child's nutrition, some of them quite intense and sarcastic. Maybe they *did* have good native herbs for treating their sickness, but I kept telling them that with decent nutrition the child would grow and maintain a degree of health. (Thomsen 1969:53)

More often than not, fieldworkers muddle through these dilemmas without resolving them in their own mind, or without effecting any lasting changes—which is not usually their purpose anyway. North Americans like to solve "needless" problems that would appear to have simple solutions if we could just get "them" to think like we do. Anthropologists sometimes feel that way too, but tend to be cautious about suggesting change because they may not have the "whole picture" and because they generally believe that the people themselves must want to change to make change effective. Also, change sometimes has unfortunate and unforeseen ramifications that negate positive change.

Laura Bohannan speaks of the tragedy of witchcraft accusation.

> I too had begun to tremble. Here it was no comfort that witches were only people. Therein lay the tragedy. These men were torn with anguish, striving to save the life of one they loved. Amara could yet live, if they could only force a confession from the witch. Each knew himself innocent. Each therefore knew the other guilty. I knew them both innocent. I watched while each strove to break the other, to force his confession, to save Amara. I knew they could not. Their battle was the more terrible for me because it was in vain and fought against shadows. ([1954] 1964:193)

There was nothing that Bohannan could do or say in this dilemma, but try to cope with her own emotions.

Thomas Belmonte found himself searching for answers to his discomfort with the level of violence he discovered in lower-class Neapolitan (Naples, Italy) families.

> Reliving the confused events of an afternoon as I wrote up my field notes became a wrenching chore. How could I record yet another exchange of insults, another bout of spitting, another discontinuous series of pecks and counterpecks? I began to block out sections of my notebook with the simple exclamation, "chaos!" which meant that the scene had flown out of control and I could no longer follow the flail of arms and fists, and the twisted, wincing faces, the curses, the grunts and the cries. (1989:79)

At times, Belmonte avoided visiting the family because he could not handle the level of violence displayed there, but at the same time he wondered if they felt that he had abandoned them because of who they were. These problems are not usually solved in any satisfactory way but linger with the outsider even after he has left the scene.

THE SHOCK OF THE NEW

We have thus far cited many of the recent ethnographies espousing the new awareness of the interactive nature of fieldwork. They possess the power to convey to us in striking and highly personal detail the raw and messy side of fieldwork; they are personal testimonies to the hold that culture has on us, our personal perseverance in the face of grave doubts, and the elusiveness of the goal of understanding the other. Although most of us will never do anthropological fieldwork, we cannot say for sure anymore where we might be living and working in the future. Even if we are not working abroad, increasingly we will encounter substantial cultural difference within our own country. For most people, daily life is likely to be less demanding and more receptive to the visitor than it is for anthropologists trying to acquire a high level of understanding. Nevertheless, more of importance can be said here about how anthropologists do fieldwork and how they feel about their experiences.

Although most successful field researchers tolerate a high level of ambiguity and uncertainty, they clearly suffer from culture shock too. As Michael Agar writes:

> The shock comes from a sudden immersion in the lifeways of a group different from yourself. Suddenly, you do not know how to interpret the stream of motions and notions that surround you. You have no idea what is expected of you. Many of the assumptions that form the bedrock of our existence are mercilessly ripped out from under you. The more you cling to them, the less you will understand about the people with whom you work. (1980:50)

Even inexperienced anthropologists are expected to know quite a bit about how cultures work before they arrive in the field, and partly because of these expectations their initial frustrations can be especially difficult to handle. In addition, fieldworkers are usually under time constraints: the time available never seems adequate to the task at hand. William Mitchell writes the following letter of frustration while in New Guinea.

> I'm spending weeks trying to figure out what any eight year old has known for several years. Now, I know why the older generation of anthropologists never accepted anyone as a bona fide anthropologist until they have been humbled by a primitive culture. It's the analogue of a didactic psychoanalysis, you're never the same again. You've been peeled, stripped and reduced to a Total Ignoramus. The level of stupidity at which I operate—even after five months here—is absolutely appalling. And I am not a bad anthropologist, but the monumental shifts it takes to apprehend the local version of reality sometimes unhinges me a bit. After all, I've usually been able to *feel* what was going on about me even if I didn't know the details of what was happening. Now I have been humbled on that one, too! (1987:104)

Fieldworkers can prepare intellectually for shock, but as Mitchell's letter so vividly shows, there is little that they can do to prepare emotionally for the experience. Shock comes in unexpected forms. Indeed, anthropologists frequently encounter reverse culture shock upon returning home from an extended stay in the field. This is an experience for which, early in their career, they are totally unprepared.

More important than the experience of shock, however, is what we make of it. Knowing that people will usually work through shock is helpful. Knowing that it will occur and knowing the symptoms forewarn us. Working through shock is aided by a good sense of humor, especially the ability to laugh at oneself (at least silently). Learning the local culture sufficiently well to predict the course of daily behavior routinizes your life and rewards you with a sense of settling in. As you begin to learn the language you begin to increase the number of your acquaintances. When you begin to know a few insiders as individuals you personalize the experience. Familiarity establishes human anchor points in a sea of strange faces. Remembering that your hosts are also going through a period of adjustment to your presence among them should take some of the sting out of your own discomfort and encourage your patience. That they need to fit your presence into their lives is important to figuring out what they are up to. They also need time to know you as a person. They may be wary of your intentions and generally suspicious as to why you are there, so it may take some time for them to trust you.

Anthropologists know that various episodes of shock (it is not necessarily a one-time experience, and it may come early, or late, or in the middle, although it is likely to come earlier than later) will challenge them to understand more about their own culture as well as the other culture. They know, too, that shock will tell them something important about their host culture. In other words, we should use the shocks and crises of fieldwork to advance our understanding, which will enhance personal adjustment. Mitchell (1987:78), although humbled at first by feelings of inadequacy, advanced personally and anthropologically when he learned why there was so much trouble over his method of paying porters in New Guinea. He had given a lump sum to the two men who organized his move to the village. They redistributed it to the porters. But the porters were angry because they did not receive more. Because of their discontent and his further inquiry, he discovered quickly that the Wape were more egalitarian that he had previously thought. Their system was more Western than he had expected. He then followed their way with success.

It is not just other cultures, of course, that we need to be tough-minded about, but also our own so that we will understand our own biases. Further, people in other cultures will have prejudged us also. This is why good fieldwork includes *productive dialogues*, the give-and-take of participant observation, between the observed and the observer.

These challenges bear obvious implications for applied programs. Imagine outsiders trying to implement programs of change in attitude and behavior, difficult under the best of circumstances, in a poorly understood population or organization. In the applied realm, anthropologists are trying to achieve a practical goal, not conducting academic research. On the other hand, applied anthropologists usually know their culture prior to launching an applied project in it. We shall return later to issues of applied anthropology.

CONCLUSION

These examples of culture shock illustrate our struggle to extend ourselves beyond the world we have created to comprehend a world created by others. We regard our sensory perceptions, language, social use of food, gender roles, and morality to be natural and fundamental to our way of life. Yet, they are likely to be among the first elements to be threatened as we experience another culture. The confrontation between "their" way and "our" way causes us to reflect on our differences. Differences may be overwhelming at first and impede our progress toward recognizing similarities. Differences are real and cannot be ignored, but common ground can still be discovered.

The experience of culture shock reveals to us two realities of human nature:

1. We live a life highly *bound* by our local cultural experience.

2. We cross our local cultural border with difficulty, but it can be crossed.

This book is about our experience, their experience, and building bridges of understanding that span the difference. It is based on the information gathered in hundreds if not thousands of ethnographies that, in turn, spring from firsthand experience in the field.

Critical Thinking

1. Did you experience culture shock in your first year of college? Examples?

2. Identify a person with whom you interact who has a different religious, cultural, class, ethnic, or racial background. How is the difference between you expressed in communicating with each other?

3. What social and cultural meanings are reflected in the preparation and consumption of food in your family? What about college?

Chapter Two

Common Ground

We seem endlessly torn between the one opinion that beneath our obviously diverse ways all human groups are really the same, and the contrary opinion that we are, in fact, as truly different as we appear to be. Anthropologists working in exotic cultures recognize the familiar even as they struggle to make sense of the strange. They despair of really comprehending another culture even as they write scientific reports on their current state of understanding. The truth is that human groups *are* fundamentally the *same*, but *also* vitally *different*. The familiar coexists with the strange. This complex reality requires that we develop a balanced view of humanity that takes into account both its universal similarities and its exotic local expressions.

Developing a comprehensive framework of cultural similarities and differences has been the continuing task of anthropology, and it is one of the principal goals of this text. This chapter presents the first part of the framework devoted to establishing our common humanity, while the following chapter is dedicated to grasping the genesis of local differences. In the present chapter we will address our common biological heritage and physical variation, the concept of culture, human thought and emotions, and ways of controlling or channeling human behavior.

We cannot properly address issues of human diversity unless we first know who we are as a species and thereby locate our common ground. To accomplish this task, we need to acquire a firm grasp of the evolutionary basis of human behavior and potential. Acquiring a firm grasp means, in this case, answering some key questions, from a comparative point of view, regarding the essential bases of cultural life. Do human groups differ in intelligence? Do some groups have superior sensory equipment? Do we all have the same emotions? How is a human self formed? What role does morality play in our lives? What role does our lived experience play in shaping our culture? How are individuals connected to groups? What is the concept of culture and how does it lead us to better insight into others and ourselves?

BRAIN, MIND, AND EVOLUTION

Compared to other animals, all normal humans are characterized by an exceptional ability to *learn*, an unparalleled faculty for *complex communication*, and a unique capacity for *self-awareness*. The critical evolutionary developments leading to these capacities are three: (1) achieving upright posture, (2) increasing the size and complexity of the brain, and (3) acquiring language. Although it remains unclear precisely what evolutionary pressures caused the emergence of bipedalism, it is clear that *Australopithecines* (prehumans found only in Africa) had achieved an upright posture by three to four million years ago. Whether upright posture was favored by a new capacity to make tools with freed hands or by a new survival ability to see over the tall grass of East Africa to search for stalking predators is not clear. A combination of these and still other unidentified forces may have formed us as bipedal creatures. What is clear is that the ability to stand on two legs preceded brain expansion and the acquisition of speech.

The second critical development was an increase in brain size, accompanied by the appearance of an expanded cerebral cortex, the outer layer of the brain and the home of higher brain functions. The brain capacity of *Australopithecines* peaked at about 475 cc, while the brain capacity of *Homo erectus*, who succeeded them, is known to run from about 775 cc to 1200 cc, or about 1000 cc on the average. This is a significant expansion over the earlier *Australopithecine* brains. The upper range of *Homo erectus* brain capacity reached nearly to the lower range of modern capacities of approximately 1200 cc to 1800 cc. Thus, fossil skulls from the *Homo erectus* era (about 500,000 to 1.6 million years ago) are much more vaulted than earlier forms in order to contain the larger brain. These fossil remains are widely distributed outside of Africa.

Frontal expansion, cranial vaulting, and the impressions left by the brain on the underside of the skull plates record the development of the cerebral cortex. Besides being the site of higher brain functions, the cortex is responsible for initiating the complex code that instructs us to push air past the pharynx to produce the sounds that are molded into speech. The expansion of the brain, clearly present in *Homo erectus*, dramatically increased our ability to learn. By the time that *Neanderthals* appeared on the scene over 100,000 years ago, (in Europe and other locations outside of Africa) brain capacities matched or exceeded the modern range. *Cro-Magnon*, the first modern human, arrived by 40,000 years ago in Europe, exhibiting fully human form and function. All human groups living today share the same brain structure and chemistry because we all derive from a common ancestor.

These developments opened us to endless possibilities. As Bernard Campbell puts it:

> Language, we can see now, was humankind's passport to a totally new level of social relationship, organization, and thought; it was the tool that allowed humans to vary expressions to meet changing conditions instead of being limited by less flexible patterns of communication, as other primates are. (1987:343)

The system of communication used by our closest primate relatives, chimpanzees, is a *signal*, or *call*, system. Call systems are closed systems that are largely restricted to signals of danger and to involuntary expressions of internal emotional and physiological states (Campbell 1987:342). They are not modified or expanded by experience over the generations, although some chimps and gorillas have, under laboratory conditions, learned an impressive number of words in American Sign Language.

Language, on the other hand, is an open system that can be expanded as experience and learning require. All human groups possess a language that is perfectly adequate to the challenges of their local neighborhood and can be adapted and expanded to changing conditions. There are no inferior or superior languages; they do what they are intended to do. In prehistoric times, language use would have supported and enhanced more complex social cooperation, thus improving our ancestors' chances for survival.

Displacement is the feature of language that allows us to speak about those conditions and objects not immediately observable to us. Through language we can displace ourselves in time and place—as this text does. Displacement means that we can dwell on our memories and plan for the future; we can think and talk about ourselves as "will be" or "have been." We can speak of faraway places. Our capacity for abstract thought allows us to be *reflective* creatures, aware of ourselves as individuals and as members of a group. The physical evolution of the brain and the development of language, then, are accompanied by an evolution of consciousness.

One critically important consequence of our evolutionary development is our increasing reliance on learning. Instead of starting off early in life with the full complement of survival behaviors generally characteristic of immature mammals, humans must learn to be competent adults over years of maturation. We are not "hard-wired" for rigid, specific response behaviors but learn from experience to modify behavior as needed. Other creatures can learn from experience too, but they are relatively restricted in this respect. Different challenges in different times and places demand that we learn new lessons as we adapt to these challenges.

We learn what we need to learn in order to survive in a particular natural and cultural environment, and this is as true today as it was millennia ago when, as fledgling humans, we first faced the ultimate problem of physical survival under harsh and demanding circumstances. We evolved as tropical creatures yet we spread rapidly into nearly every climatic region in the world.

Today, we face equally challenging problems of how we are to survive the consequences of those early successes. Clearly, one of the lessons we have not learned so well is how to get along with each other. A key element in dispelling myth and prejudice about each other is to appreciate the universal role of experience and interest, however different, in shaping human perceptions, thoughts, and feelings.

SOCIAL RACE

Cultural difference is not based on racial difference. There is no innate relationship between race and behavior or values. Various forms of prejudice and discrimination frequently posit close relationships among race and intelligence and morality, but these are sociological issues. *Social race* refers to the fact that people use culturally and socially constructed labels to identify groups thought to be races. As Conrad Kottak (2001) observes, a child born of a mixed black and white marriage in North America will be arbitrarily labeled black, although that label does not fit biological reality. In North America, one is either black or white; in Brazil, there are many categories between these polar opposites that recognize various shades of mixture. They, too, are arbitrary categories with little meaning except for what people want to make of them sociologically.

Humans no doubt have been aware of physical differences as long as they have existed. Whether perceived differences had any particular meaning for early humans is unknown. Throughout much of history, cultural and religious differences appear to have been more important than differences in physical appearance. The *extensive* and *systematic* racism, with themes of innate and fixed superiority and inferiority, which we observe in the world today and in our recent past is linked with the rise of colonialism and slavery in the West.

The act of classifying anything requires establishing criteria by which to do so. The common criteria used by Westerners for centuries to sort humans into racial categories are skin color, nose form, hair form, shape of the skull, and height. In their eagerness to achieve their scientific mission of describing cultures and peoples of the world, anthropologists at one time also used these criteria, but without the assumption of fixed and inherited ability. In the 1960s, however, anthropologists became increasingly wary of racial classification and ceased constructing their own classifications. There are a number of reasons for becoming uneasy about racial classification.

One reason for scientific discomfort is that the commonly used criteria do not present themselves to us in neat packages as stereotypes suggest. Knowing the skin color of a group tells us nothing with certainty about its hair or nose form. If one were to map independently each criterion as it appears around the world, much like the clinal variations in temperature on a weather map, one would observe areas of overlap among traits, but also large areas where they do not *covary*. We would be better off predicting the weather from the variables of temperature and barometric pressure than we would predicting a racial stereotype. Making such a map of racial traits is called *clinal analysis*, and the resulting mismatch of popular racial traits—independent variation rather than covariation—is known as *discordance*. Some native peoples in the western desert of Australia, for example, have very dark skin, but blonde, or "tawny," hair. Clinal analysis undermines racial stereotyping.

A second problem is that there is little demonstrated scientific reason for designing a racial classification, even for biological or medical reasons. We know that darker skin provides superior protection against skin cancer (because it filters out harmful ultraviolet rays) and that taller, thinner people survive better in the desert, while shorter and more compactly built people do better in the Arctic (because of their differential ability to dissipate or conserve heat). These are cases of climatic engineering that give us clues for the manufacture of difference. But we quickly run out of other reasons for classification. African Americans and Africans, particularly from West Africa, display a high incidence, 25 percent to 40 percent in some areas, of sickle-cell anemia (oxygen-starved red blood cells become misshapen, and infected people die early in life if untreated), but so do some Mediterranean European populations (as well as those in other geographical regions). A study of this illness would cut across European, African, and African American populations.

A third argument against racial classification is that it assumes the existence of pure races, which in fact probably has never been the case. It should be noted, too, that there has never been any solid evidence that blending races has any deleterious effect; if anything, the result of interracial marriage is that it usually produces children of ability equal with or superior to that of the parents. In any case, racial mixture has been common since ancient times.

For these reasons, and still others, race is a scientifically discredited concept. Yet, the term persists in everyday language because of habit and because of the mistaken belief that race is an easily observable reality of everyday life. More important, race persists because it is used politically, socially, and economically to distinguish groups of people from each other, to the disadvantage of some. Therefore the term has great social significance, and for this reason race is best defined as a *social construction*.

THOUGHT, EMOTIONS, AND CULTURE

Perception and Cognition

The key to understanding perception and cognition cross-culturally lies in acquiring knowledge of how a people are socialized to think about their social and natural environments. *Perception refers to the process of receiving and organizing sensory data at a primary level.* The same physical universe of sensations binds all human groups. All humans lack the biological capability to see ultraviolet rays or hear a dog-whistle, and have a comparatively poor sense of smell. But we are driven by our intelligence to make sense of what we do perceive. We are intellectually aggressive; we reach out to seize nature and to organize it conceptually in a manner that makes sense to us. What makes sense to a specific group of people is to be found in their local experience.

Outsiders initially lack the knowledge to understand local perceptions but often make their ethnocentric judgments anyway. For example, early European explorers, colonial administrators, and missionaries lacked knowledge of the peoples they contacted, but this ignorance usually did not prevent them from making unenlightened judgments. Moreover, they often had little real interest in discovering the "native view" and thus tended to end their travels as bound by their own world as if they had never sailed the ocean. The combination of their Eurocentric attitude toward non-Western peoples and their ignorance of other ways of life generated a number of negative stereotypes of other peoples. Westerners indulged themselves in a number of fallacies such as a belief in the "primitive mind," or a savage "sixth sense." Many believed that native peoples were simply "superstitious children." The latter belief conveniently supported the dominating and paternalistic stance of Westerners toward those whom they subjugated. On the other hand, native peoples had their own ignorance and stereotypes about Westerners. But the brain is the same for all normal humans, while the mind varies as a product of the brain's interaction with experience and culture in specific settings.

Many cross-cultural studies have substantiated the critical role of local experiences in producing different performances on tests of perception and cognition. Anthropologists often cite examples of differ-

ences in perception. We have already seen that Alverson failed to read
the story of the sands because she had no relevant experience. A native
child could read a spoor much better than she. On the other hand, her
hosts would have equal difficulty functioning in a technologically
sophisticated city. Turnbull (1962:263) tells of being accompanied by
the forest pygmies to distant savannas. Emerging from the dense forest, they saw for the first time buffalo grazing in the distance. The pygmies, who had lived their entire lives cloistered by the thick rainforest
that enveloped them, asked Turnbull about the curious "insects" in
front of them. They did not understand that these buffalo were much
larger than they appeared to be because they could not conceptually
compensate for the effect of distance on their perception of size. This
misperception is not an example of primitive mentality, but the work of
life experience.

John Berry (1976) was able to relate the different performances of
Inuit (Eskimos of Baffin Island) and Temne (West Africa) on tests of
spatial perception to both the local ecology and child-rearing practices.
He concluded that both perception and child rearing are adaptive, and
not a series of random choices. The Inuit are hunters in a snow-clad
environment, which, to outsiders, is read as a featureless world of
white. They must be able to find their way around this world; they must
be acutely aware of fine details. The Inuit train their children for independence by stressing personal skills, self-reliance, and individualism.
These child-rearing practices have survival value and correlate generally with a high degree of spatial awareness and visual discrimination.
The Temne, on the other hand, are sedentary farmers surrounded by
richly detailed vegetation. Their survival does not depend on making
fine distinctions in their natural environment. Temne child-rearing
practices stress relationships of dependency, which correlates with less
spatial discrimination and awareness. The difference between the two
groups is related to significantly different sets of natural challenges
and cultural solutions. Cultural differences and perception styles
emerge from meeting those challenges. We issue the caveat here that
environment does not determine culture; it only limits possibilities,
especially where groups have limited technology.

Two ethnographic studies of the senses have jolted anthropologists into the realization that they have been largely ignorant of how
cultures systematically shape sensory data. Paul Stoller's (1989) study
of the Songhay of Niger deals more generally with the senses, while
Steven Feld's (1990) ethnography focuses on the sound system, both
natural and human, of the Kaluli of Papua New Guinea. Stoller is particularly critical of Western scientific empiricism that "focuses" on the
sense of vision, the gaze, as a primary metaphor for knowing. The term
observation connotes gazing. He suggests that a historical shift, the scientific revolution and its stress on scientific observation, accounts for

this emphasis. However, the principal point here is that Westerners are predisposed to stress the visual while other cultures may stress other senses, as Feld's work on sound demonstrates. We will return to Feld later in this chapter.

Western concepts of linear time are not shared necessarily by other cultures. When outsiders and insiders act on the basis of different assumptions about time, misunderstanding and irritation frequently arise. Space, time, and social relationships can merge into one unfamiliar category in some cultures. Laura Bohannan ([1954] 1964:52) was asked to accompany some informants on a visit to relatives. When she asked how long the trip would take in order to know whether to pack a lunch, she was told that it would be some distance. Believing it would be perhaps a half-day's walk, she packed a lunch, only to arrive at their destination in less than an hour. Later, she realized that her informants were speaking in kinship terms of social distance rather than geographical distance. They were "distant" relatives living close. She had not misunderstood what they said, but what they meant—distance measured in social terms.

Cognition is the process of gaining, storing, and using knowledge. Cognition, too, is best understood as shaped by experience and interests. Puzzled by certain test results on stimulus orientation between English and Zambian children, Robert Serpell (1971a, 1971b) devised a culturally sensitive test. Whereas earlier studies revealed no difference in performance on simple stimuli, they did show a difference on more complex stimuli patterns. Curious, Serpell decided to give three separate tasks to the children. Children in both groups were accustomed to modeling clay, and so both were given such a test. Because the Zambian children were also accustomed to wire modeling, and the English children to copying figures with pencil and paper, Serpell added these tasks to the first. Both groups did well on the clay task, with which they had common experience, and each did well on its particular, accustomed task. Neither group, however, did as well as the other on the task that was new to it. Each group performed best on that task with which it had experience, and poorly on the unfamiliar one. This study illustrates the role of experience in cognition, and warns against naive cross-cultural testing.

Cognitive anthropology is devoted to discovering how cultures and subcultures organize, store, and apply their knowledge. A classic ethnography in this vein is James Spradley's ([1970] 2000) work with alcoholics on skid row, where he elicits from his informants their organization of experience centered on drinking and being jailed for public drunkenness. Another example of a cognitive approach is Agar's (1973) study of heroin addicts' organization of a world centered on getting and using heroin. Although these two studies take as their subjects people who are uniquely dedicated to one consuming task, getting and staying drunk or getting and staying high, they bear vivid testimony to the human ability to integrate intellect, experience, and interest and to focus subsequent action. The individuals in these groups are organizing and naming their world for reasons that are important to them. If we can understand what motivates people to act and to organize intellectually their world in a certain way, we can better understand their behavior.

Tests of perception and cognition developed in the West have been administered frequently in other cultures with varying results. These tests are, however, quite treacherous when given cross-culturally. It is especially important, first, to understand that they are often given to people with no experience, or particular motivation, in taking such tests. Second, the tests are typically developed and "normed" in Western culture and applied in a non-Western culture. Thus, they often involve tasks that do not translate well in another culture. Therefore we must be particularly careful about the assumptions behind the tests and the conclusions we draw from their results.

The administration and interpretation of tests cross-culturally should be accompanied by a sound knowledge of the cultural context. Michael Cole and Barbara Means (1981:54) point out how daunting it is to discover the variables that explain observed behavior when the experience of the investigators and that of the subjects are significantly different. Indeed, Cole makes the same point about intracultural tests of cognition. Even within our own culture we are testing persons of a different age, a different gender, a different social class, or a different ethnic group than that of the researcher. How well does the observer know these worlds? How well does she see their world from their point of view? Devising and interpreting cross-cultural tests is like traversing what appears to be solid common ground only to discover it pitted with pockets of intellectual quicksand. A valid test can only rest on solid knowledge of the group tested.

It is well known by now that standard tests of intelligence are culture bound, and gender and social-class biased. They are effective in predicting how well one will do in formal schooling, which is what they were primarily designed to do. As Stephen Gould (1981) details in his study of the development and early use of Binet's intelligence test, the test was born of the practical need of the French government to identify those children in public school who required remedial education. It was not an application flowing from a specific theory of intelligence; it was almost immediately misused to label negatively those children who did poorly on it. In North America, H. H. Goddard and Lewis Terman who were interested in showing intelligence to be fixed and distributed unequally through the population popularized Binet's test. Popular acceptance of the test was speeded when R. M. Yerkes launched massive testing of over 1.5 million recruits in World War I. Unfortunately, the results seemed to indicate that virtually half of the white recruits were functioning morons, while recent immigrants and blacks did even worse (Gould 1981:223). Although this finding was due to serious flaws in the test and its application, alarmists, fearing depletion of genetic purity in the United States, used the results to push through Congress legislation to restrict immigration, especially from non-Western European countries.

The use of intelligence tests to document innate differences between various racial and ethnic groups still emerges from time to time in spite of all the resulting problems. It should be emphasized that the tests themselves are influenced by experience, both in their construction and scoring, and in the responses of the subjects who take the test. Gould (1981:176) cites an example of a question Terman added to Binet's original list. An American Indian, in town for the first time in his life, observed a white man riding down the street. The American Indian said that the white man was lazy for walking sitting down. Terman's question was, "What was the white man riding?" Terman only accepted bicycle as the answer—not cars because the driver's legs did not go up and down, nor horses because a American Indian would know a horse. Nor would he accept a person in a wheel chair or someone riding on another person's back. The American Indian was wrong because he didn't answer bicycle. Other questions had to do with cultural items also, such as identifying a baseball player, something an immigrant would have difficulty doing. These are questions of *culture content*, not intelligence.

Whenever such tests are administered in populations with a different experience, for example those lacking experience in formal schooling, the results are likely to be invalid and interpretations suspect. Indeed, the more Western schooling that non-Western groups have, the better they do on these tests, because their experience more closely matches the experience on which the tests are based (Cole et al. 1971). Individuals vary widely in abilities and aptitudes in any culture, but there appears to be no significant difference in intellectual ability among groups cross-culturally.

From this discussion of perception and cognition we can derive three principles:

1. All humans live in the same perceptual world and have the same basic cognitive capacity.

2. The specific organization and use of knowledge in a particular culture relates more to the experience, interests, and challenges perceived by the members of that culture than it does to those of another culture. The second principle suggests the third, one of discovery.

3. We will discover the key to understanding another culture in the experience and interests of that culture.

These principles advance our understanding of similarities and differences because they identify simultaneously our shared inheritance and our lived difference. All groups begin life with the same "equipment," but different experiences in different neighborhoods of the world forge different lifeways and different ways of seeing the world.

Emotions

Culture constructs a world of feelings characteristic of individuals and groups. While specialists disagree over exactly how many emotions humans have, there is a much wider agreement on a common core of five: (1) Fear is an important emotion because of its ability to warn us of threat and to focus our attention; it has obvious survival value. (2) The feeling of attachment is quite understandable in a social species. (3) Having feelings of attachment necessarily sets us up for the feeling of loss, or grief. (4) Anger is clearly universal. (5) What we call happiness or joy certainly is a candidate. Beyond these universal five, the list becomes more contentious.

We shall take the same perspective on emotions that we did with perception and cognition. We all share a common capacity for a variety of emotions regardless of how they are expressed, valued, or named in a particular culture. There is good evidence (Ekman 1982:128–143) that people from different cultures can read with fair accuracy the display of many emotions registered on the faces of people in other cultures. But much more study is required on this subject before firm conclusions can be reached. We should recall that facial displays and body language fall into the realm of observable behavior; the hard part is guessing what is going on behind the display. Like responses to tests of perception and cognition, the display may have many antecedent causes. The actor, for example, might actually be masking her "true" emotions. Robert Levy (1973:97–98) tells of the distrust that early visitors expressed toward Tahitians because they never knew what they were feeling by looking at their faces. Westerners interpreted Tahitian facial displays as deceptive and thus the people as insincere; the Tahitians, on the other hand, thought it too disruptive to the group to wear visibly one's emotions in public like Westerners do. Social grace and cohesion are valued over personal expressiveness.

One of the major problems in dealing with emotions cross-culturally lies in language translation. The central issue is that we impose the discrete categories of language on what appears to be complex and ambiguous natural phenomena. If we translate emotion words from another language, for example love and anger, are they different words for the same emotions, or do they in fact denote different emotions? Catherine Lutz (1988) offers an example of the problems inherent in translating emotion words. The Ifaluk use the term *fago* to refer to what we might call love. Lutz, however, suggests that the social implications of fago and love are different. Fago does not suggest the primary sexual, romantic aspect that love does in our terms. Instead, fago entails a caring and responsibility, even sadness, for those less fortunate than the giver of fago (p. 119). It suggests a hierarchical relationship not present in our conception of love. She further notes that *song*, justifiable anger, is centered on moral violations of personal relationships (p. 155), while anger in mainstream North American culture arises most often over the constraint and frustration of individuality (p. 231). A strict translation of fago and song into English equivalents would therefore be misleading.

The issue of translation is not simply semantic carping; love and anger really are different in Ifaluk culture. Here we face the question of properly weighing the general against the particular—the question of a balanced perspective mentioned earlier. Which alternative we choose depends on the question being asked. The first question is the universal one: do all humans have the capacity for anger? The answer is clearly yes. The second question has to do with how anger is defined, induced, used, and expressed in a particular culture. The first question addresses our commonality, but it is cast at such a general level of understanding that, while crucial to constructing a basic framework for understanding, it is ultimately too abstract to help us grasp important local meanings. Indeed, it is the local meaning of concepts that constantly defies our understanding. The local stamp of experience on emotions is tremendously important. If we think that our love is the same as Ifaluk love, and act accordingly in Ifaluk culture, it could get us into trouble, because the two loves carry different implications for social interaction.

When we name emotions we may feel that we are simply referring to what is naturally within all of us, a concrete entity called anger, for example. With this assumption in our unconscious mind we are apt to reason that they feel just like we do: every human knows what anger is regardless of its name, we might argue. But we have seen that this is only true in the general sense. This argument is another example of the fallacy of naive realism. That is, the belief that emotion is so basic to our species that we are all alike in this respect. The case of song suggests otherwise. Naive realism does not account for the power of local culture to mold the emotional norms of a group in dramatically different ways. Even within our own culture individuals sometimes find it difficult to empathize with another person's anger when shared experience is lacking.

Each culture values an *emotional style*: normative ideas about what kinds of emotions there are, when to express them, and with what intensity (Middleton 1989). As individuals growing up in a particular culture we learn an emotional style, part of which is usually governed by gender identity. In the United States, men are traditionally not supposed to cry except under certain unusual conditions; women are expected to cry more often. Emotional style is part of our identity and motivates us to act. A display or a statement of anger defines who you think you are both as an individual and as a member of a group. Ilongot men who hunt heads because of their grief and anger are making both individual and group statements (Rosaldo 1989:3).

Culture

Naive realism underestimates the degree to which learning a culture defines the borders of our lives. To recognize our naiveté is to peel back another layer of our own culture, the inner layers of which are home to our deeply implicit, unconsciously held, culturally shaped assumptions about the way the world works. These assumptions, values, and ideas may rest concealed and undisturbed until challenged by an alternative reality. Even at the point of challenge we may not know the source of our uneasiness. Alverson was fortunate that her hosts were willing to speak so freely with her about their own assumptions regarding hospitality and serving kadi, in contrast to Fernea's experience in Marrakech where she never discovered why she was told to ignore the injured man in the street.

Culture is *learned* behavior; nearly all of human behavior is learned, excepting of course basic biological functions. The roots of the term culture are in French and Latin with connotations of nurturing and growing. Learning is a process of growing that needs nurturing. We learn ways of thinking, feeling, and seeing; we learn morals and meaning, and the practical arts of everyday life. While we do respond to the press of biological drives (for example, hunger and thirst), our responses are culturally guided. We can learn to control pain as do ritual fire walkers, yogis, and dancers of the Sun Dance (Williams 1983:161–171). The detailed cultural acts of our lives are not guided by genetic programming to the degree experienced by other social creatures. This fact leaves us with great flexibility of behavior by which to cope with rapidly changing circumstances. In terms of evolution we are generalized creatures whose survival depends on flexible behavior.

While we stress the important role of flexible behavior, we need at the same time to acknowledge that we obviously also inherit at least general capacities for behavior that undergird specific behavior. Language, culture, and emotions are examples of the interaction between inherited capacities and learned behavior. Precisely where we will ultimately find the proper balance between inheritance (nature) and learned behavior (nurture) remains to be discovered.

In the early part of the twentieth century when anthropology was establishing itself largely on the basis of the concept of culture and its priority in explaining diverse ways of life, a hard distinction was often made between instinct and learned behavior. It was necessary to point out that cultural variation could not be accounted for by reference to instinct, a constant, because a particular set of instincts is characteristic of a species. In other words, if humans are one species, and therefore possess but one set of instincts, how could behavior vary cross-culturally?

Behavior that varies cross-culturally is, in the old way of thinking, evidence against the operation of instinct. Thus, for almost every proposed instinct, anthropologists discovered exceptions in the actual practice of a specific group of people. An instinct for survival is negated by the widespread act of suicide for personal and cultural reasons. An instinctual incest taboo (although a nearly universal cultural value) is negated by actual practice in most societies. Instincts for aggression and territoriality have not been substantiated. So where are those instincts? We know today that the crude dichotomy between instinct and learned behavior inaccurately reflects the complex reality that actually exists between genome and behavior (Konner 1982). Specialists in evolutionary psychology and sociobiology are currently working on this relationship, but we cannot properly deal with this complex issue here.

We can, on the other hand, state with a high degree of confidence that variations in human behavior are not attributable to differences in "race." As we saw earlier, race is not a biological reality. Geographical variations give rise to superficial differences in size, shape, and color, and have nothing to do with social, moral, or intellectual capacity (Gould 1981, Molnar 1983). An infant from any group can be taken from one culture and placed in another and do perfectly well in the new culture, provided that he has an equal opportunity. In this sense, humans are completely interchangeable.

Human behavior is largely learned behavior, and it is learned only in the company of other humans. Because we are born immature social creatures, there is no other way of acquiring culture than in the presence of other humans. Just how critical this requirement of social learning is can be driven home by considering the negative case of children who are isolated from the nurturing presence of other humans. Children who have been locked away in closets, attics, and basements at an early age, depending on the timing and severity of their experience, do not speak, or walk, or have any conception of themselves aside from being a crude bundle of drives and reflexes. Lacking the power of language, they have no sense of self, or personhood. Without language they can learn little of their culture or of themselves. Depending on specific conditions, these children, when given remedial instruction, learn slowly and are always intellectually behind others of their chronological age.

Specific cultures are not biologically inherited and therefore must be *acquired* by each child by the process of *socialization*, or *culture transmission*, from one generation to the next. This process both preserves the continuity of a culture and turns succeeding generations of individuals into culturally competent adults. The succeeding generation receives the hard-won experience and knowledge of preceding generations. Most native peoples, for example, can name and use hundreds of species of plants, animals, birds, and fish. This is survival knowledge accumulated over generations of experience and experimentation; it could not be duplicated in a single generation without learning from others.

The combination of accumulated experience and flexible behavior enhances our chances of surviving challenging conditions. For this reason, culture is said to be *adaptive*. We learn a culture so well that much of our behavior subsequently becomes *habitual* and *unconscious*. Individually, we *internalize* culture, which means that we accept it for ourselves and commit to it emotionally and intellectually. When we internalize a culture, we do not easily give it up.

The routine satisfaction that we derive from our culture normally outweighs occasional dissatisfaction and makes it painful for us at times to change. The world our culture constructs for us is so familiar that it seems to be the "right" or "natural" way of life. Because of our comfort in tradition and frequent discomfort with change, our flexible behavior often becomes inflexible. All cultures seem to suffer at times from this tension between old and new. This does not mean that we all become robots incapable of change, only that routine can be comfortable.

Effective group life depends on learning a common culture and *sharing* common understandings and expectations. One of the roles of socialization is to instill in children the accepted customs of the group. Although socialization is not a perfect process producing identical social persons, it does well in coordinating individuality. Humans do vary individually in temperament and aptitude, and these characteristics interact with cultural values and norms. In the words of Anthony Wallace ([1961] 1970:23), socialization does not "replicate uniformity, but organizes diversity." We are individuals living in groups; we are not cultural clones.

In spite of the general effectiveness of socialization, culture is not shared perfectly. Culture is based on a sharing sufficient for us to work effectively as a group. Even in simply organized bands of forty to sixty individuals (sometimes called egalitarian societies) males and females do not share culture completely because of gender distinctions. Generational difference also leads to incomplete sharing. Age and sex are, in fact, two universal features of human life that result in a differential sharing of culture. As we came to live in ever larger and more complex groups, greater internal differences developed that led to various forms of social differentiation. The different life chances, for example, of those in various social classes in this country have been well documented for decades (Sennett and Cobb 1973). Those in the lower social class are more likely to experience crime, disease, poor schooling, and contact with welfare agencies than those in the middle and upper classes.

Cultures are systems of meaning and symbols (Geertz 1973). As we shall see later, we attach meaning to acts, things, and nature. Body adornment, hair style, and body language all have meaning. Burning the American flag is a symbolic act. The flag is a symbol whose mainstream meaning is known to all, but contested by some. That is, to some it is a symbol of freedom, to others it is a symbol of oppression. Burning it is to some an unpatriotic act, to others it is an act of supreme patriotism. Symbols have an arbitrary, not fixed, meaning.

Subcultures, customs and beliefs that overlap with but depart significantly from the mainstream culture, emerge in nations for various sociological and historical reasons. Class, ethnicity, and perceived race are common sources of differential socialization. Subculture formation is most often understood as partly self-generated and partly imposed by a dominant culture on the basis of perceived difference. However, a subculture is not merely a collection of different customs and beliefs, nor is it an incompetent imitation of mainstream culture. It is organized, systematic, and does not seek to imitate. Yet, it remains with one foot in the mainstream culture. These are important issues that we will revisit in the following chapter.

Language acquisition is a critical and integral part of socialization. Without it, we cannot participate effectively in human life. Imagine the dark and lonely world of Helen Keller, blind and deaf at birth, before she discovered language. The presence of language, and her eventual mastery of it, freed her from this dark world because she had gained the means of knowing herself and the world around her. She finally was able to establish nurturing relationships with others. A problem in either socialization or language acquisition usually affects the other because of this close interdependency, as Keller's case illustrates.

CHANNELING BEHAVIOR

Another way of looking at socialization is to see it as coordinating individual and group goals and means. Ideally, by the time a child reaches adulthood she has internalized the values, goals, and procedures accepted in her culture. Having internalized these *mores*, the person is able to be self-monitoring, acting in culturally consistent ways with little external prompting from others. In the process of learning her culture, the child also learns her identity and the roles she will be expected to play in life. Children are, in fact, generally taught what they need to know in order to be competent adults, as the cases of Temne and Inuit child-rearing practices substantiate.

Socialization and Social Identity

Socialization is a life-long passage and not limited simply to childhood. It is so important that most cultures in the world ritually mark the more important transitions in the life cycle. These rituals come under the general label of *rites of passage* (Van Gennep 1908). Life cycle events such as birth, transition to adulthood, marriage, and death are the most commonly recognized events. Human groups have a vested interest in channeling and marking life cycle events because they are particularly important to both the group and the individual. These events are foci of conflict and tension and therefore require an orderly handling to avoid unnecessary friction. They serve to define new statuses and to prescribe new rights and duties for the individuals entering a new stage.

The initiation rites common among native peoples usually involve prior instruction in the beliefs and morals of the group as well as the ceremony that marks the passage of adolescents into adulthood. In secular North America, formal education and graduation act much like rites of passage, although some particular religious observances of transitions, such as confirmation and *bar mitzvah*, remain. Extending formal education into college and beyond blurs the change to adulthood (Moffatt 1989). Partly for this reason, the transition from adolescence to adulthood in mainstream American culture, compared to many other cultures, is poorly marked and delays recognition and responsibility as an adult.

Socialization turns raw humans into social persons, who then interact with each other on the basis of their social identities. Note that the Panare had trouble deciding who Dumont was, and therefore how to interact with him. On the other side, Dumont struggled with the question of how to present himself to the Panare. When Dumont became a "brother," his role-status-identity was established and his interaction with them better defined. Even in North America, with its stress on individuality, ambiguous identity, role, and status affect relationships adversely. Such problems are particularly evident in cases of sociocultural change where roles and identities are being redefined. For example, the feminist movement, where women are seeking to redefine their traditional identity and to reassess their role in contemporary North American life, creates ambiguity at times for both women and men, with consequences for the quality of their interaction with each other.

Role, Status, and Self

A social system can be seen as an organization of roles and statuses. A *role* refers to the behavior that a particular social person is expected to display. A role entails certain rights and duties. Parents have both rights over and responsibilities to children. A *status* is a recognized position in the social system. Roles accompany statuses. It is useful to conceive of roles as coming in pairs. Each role has a *comple-*

ment, for example, parent–child, teacher–student, husband–wife. Complementarity can also be seen working in culture change as women seek to redefine their identity and role in contemporary life, they necessarily call into question the traditional role and identity of men as well.

The idea of role is drawn from the theater. A theatrical role is a script that has already been written by the playwright and then played or interpreted by actors. Each actor plays the role in a recognizable but individual way. No two actors will play a role in the same way. The same is true in life. We are born into a world already made, roles already prescribed, and we learn to fit into those roles. We will play many roles in our lifetime, but none of us will play the same role exactly the way another person will. The role of teacher is played competently by almost all qualified individuals, but with considerable individual variation within normal limits. Just because we fit generally into roles, however, does not mean that we also do so comfortably. Most of us, in all cultures, feel at least occasional discomfort in established roles.

The concept of *self* is useful in making a distinction between role and player (Erchak 1992). The self is a conscious, reflective, and interpreting person. The self is the public person. The conscious self is aware of his daily performance in roles, and the self monitors this performance constantly. Thus, the self reflects on his activities and the responses of others. The self interprets situations for their relevance to his own actions, which the self may modify because of his interpretation. This view underscores both the dynamic, process-oriented nature of the self and the self-monitoring function of properly socialized individuals. Acknowledging individual social awareness also balances the basic characterization of humans as simply habitual, unconscious social actors, which the internalized culture perspective seems to suggest. In addition, it counters the popular misconception of "natives" as unthinking slaves to their customs. We all are both *habitual and conscious actors*.

Role definition has a political side to it. Who defines roles? Who defines identity? In a sense we all do because we approve and disapprove, reward and punish role performance. We all are agents of social control. Yet, American Indians, African Americans, women, and other minorities are acutely aware of the fact that master roles tend to be defined by those who are in power (Carmichael and Hamilton 1967). They know that terms like "Indians," "Negroes," and "girls" identify them in negative ways that serve dominant power interests. These terms carry with them much biased and self-serving baggage, and their connotative meaning implies a lesser social status. Efforts to change negative public perceptions of minorities often include, but are certainly not limited to, changing negative labels that imply a stereotyped behavior. We will return to these issues later.

Anthropologists working in another culture cannot entirely avoid having to cope with the indigenous role system. The Ferneas, Obolers, and Alversons were learning this lesson as they settled into their host culture. The statement by Hoyt Alverson that they were becoming a Tswana couple is both accurate and revealing. In order to participate effectively, they had to adjust to existing expectations, at least to a minimally acceptable degree. By conforming to these expectations they learned more about the host culture than if they had chosen to go their own way. "Fitting-in" is part of the research strategy. Some cultures force the outsider to a strict conformity, but others permit more room for negotiation. Thus, if we as outsiders declare our independence from the indigenous role system, we will learn less by doing so (recall Laura Bohannan's ambivalence about being accepted and losing her independent, privileged role).

Morality

Morality is a learned behavior. All cultures create value hierarchies out of their experience and interest. Morality refers to those values at the top of the hierarchy, which are set aside and awarded additional importance. Morality implies emotional commitment, as well as the threat of punishment, to a set of values; otherwise the incentive to adhere to valued behavior would be weak. Commitment to morality creates an internal drive to the right behavior that is of obvious value in maintaining social cohesion.

Morality is integrated with the principal elements and issues of a culture. Among the Taita of Kenya, males are scrutinized through the years for their ability to construct a "moral career," and thus to achieve an honored elderhood. Most important in this career is their handling of anger, particularly in performing *kutasa*, an anger removal rite. The rite consists of making a declaration of anger and expelling fluid from the mouth, thus "casting out anger" (Harris 1978:138–140). The purpose of the rite is to cleanse the person, males most importantly, of the feeling of anger. It is both a personal and a social act. By executing kutasa, he makes his anger a public affair, which involves others in solving the problem. In resolving the conflict, the community reasserts moral values, and reinforces group identity. If a male is known to harbor anger, but will not confess it through kutasa, he suffers a negative mark against his moral career, and against his very identity as a Taita male. In this single example, role, morality, gender, group identity, and the channeling of emotions are all demonstrated.

CONCLUSION

Humans evolved as one species sharing the same perceptual, cognitive, and emotional capacities. We survive on the basis of our ability to learn rapidly, to communicate complex ideas, and to transmit our knowledge to succeeding generations. Culture is learned behavior, constrained by inherited capacities that give general directions for specific and flexible behavior. Culture refers to values, ideas, expectations, things we make, clothing we wear, behavior we express. Culture shapes how we see things, what we make of what we see, and how we feel about it. We adapt to different environments and situations through culture. We survive with culture, but perish without it.

Because individuals are born without detailed genetic programming for behavior, and because of our extended period of immaturity, we place a premium on learning during the socialization process. We learn our culture, and we learn who we are. We learn personal and group identity and prepare ourselves to assume roles as competent adults. These roles are culturally defined. We learn those morals and values that help us to define who we are and that guide our behavior along expected and appropriate channels.

All human groups possess a similar capacity to learn from experience and to create solutions to local challenges. All ways of life that exist or have existed constitute experiments in survival, but it is doubtful that any have failed because of the innate inferiority of a people. Diversity sprouts from common fertile ground. Raising boys and girls differently is a form of diversity; living in different cultures or different social classes are forms of diversity. Being physically or mentally challenged is a form of diversity. A complex organization of differentiated roles and experiences creates diversity. The borders of small worlds of experience are as vigorously defended as the borders of large ones. It is difficult for residents of the different worlds to communicate with each other across these borders. These experiential worlds, cross-cultural or intracultural, can be difficult to escape and equally difficult to enter, but continuing to skirmish only on their peripheries frustrates our discovery of common ground.

The key to unraveling human diversity, and crossing the borders of our own world, is to be found in probing the experience and interest of another group as filtered through those aspects of culture discussed in this chapter.

Critical Thinking

1. How do interests, experience, and intelligence relate to each other?

2. Take any of the basic emotions, say anger or joy. Think about what actions or situations trigger that emotion in you. Does this reaction characterize you as a unique individual, a member of a gender, a member of a social class, or other group?

3. The best way to begin to understand another people's cognitive framework, or emotional style is by _____.

Chapter Three

Our Lived Difference

Simply being tolerant of diversity because it makes us feel good momentarily or because it is politically correct is a counterfeit tolerance. Without appropriate information and perspective, this stance leaves us poorly prepared to withstand ignorant but heated and biased assertions about other groups. It leaves us awash in the dangerously shifting currents so characteristic of issues of diversity. Arming ourselves instead with solid information, proven perspectives, and sharp analysis will better prepare us to handle the problem at hand, which in this chapter is to understand why and how diversity emerges from our basic similarities.

Differences develop out of the fact that we live our lives in different places, different times, and different circumstances. We live in different neighborhoods of the world. We know our own neighborhood exceedingly well, but we know little of other neighborhoods. When, as distant observers, we see behavior in other neighborhoods that we do not understand we try nevertheless to make sense of it. The act of interpreting and assigning meaning to alien behavior draws from our experience in our own neighborhood, and that experience may be irrelevant to the one observed. Our interpretation is biased from the outset, even we don't intend it to be.

We counter this local bias by extending the framework begun in the last chapter, where we established our commonality. We know that we must place behavior in its context, but now we can be more specific about how to do this. Three basic perspectives on culture will help us: (1) culture as *adaptation*; (2) culture as *meaning*; and (3) culture as *system*. They are not the only perspectives that yield insights into other cultures, but they will provide us with a satisfactory, if rudimentary, foundation upon which to build further insights.

47

CULTURE AS ADAPTATION

We have already defined culture as learned beliefs and behavior, and noted that most of human behavior is learned within yet-to-be defined inherited capacities. We further noted that we learn culture so well and so early in our lives that it becomes largely unconscious routine. Moreover, culture must be shared sufficiently well among members of a society to ensure a minimal level of survival. Every day in countless ways we reproduce and reaffirm our culture by living it. Our daily behavior continues our culture, expresses it, and reinforces it. Culture accumulates over generations so that knowledge is not relearned by each generation for the group as a whole, although, of course, maturing children must learn their culture in order to become competent adults. Finally, culture is *adaptive*; we literally *learn* to survive in various localities and historical circumstances.

Whether finch, or human, all species have adaptive characteristics that permit them to survive in their particular environment. The differing sizes and shapes of the beaks of finches in the Galapagos Islands impressed the observant Charles Darwin and played a vital role in his formulation of the theory of evolution by means of natural selection. Variations in beak size and shape are adaptive—uniquely shaped to acquire particular food resources—to the many microenvironments in the Galapagos Islands (off the coast of Ecuador) and on the mainland of South America where the finches are also found.

These are biological adaptive mechanisms. Although we have described some of the superficial physical differences among humans (such as skin color) as adaptive in ancient times, to specific environments, we actually are able to live in a wide variety of environments today regardless of skin color because of our ability to adapt through the use of culture. Culture is our adaptive mechanism. Our ability to learn quickly from experience and to mitigate the direct effect of the environment (clothing, shelter, fire, space shuttle) on our physical selves extends our adaptive range to a wide variety of environments, some quite harsh.

By the time of our emergence in fully human form and function, at least 40,000 years ago, we had come to rely heavily on our unparalleled ability to learn the requisite survival skills to live in quite hostile environments. Millennia ago we learned how to domesticate plants and animals, and this knowledge profoundly changed the human experience. We dramatically increased our food supply, settled down, and lived in larger settlements. We domesticated plants and animals long before we discovered the science of genetics. We learned instead by the panhuman processes of trial-and-error, and observation. We transmitted our slowly accumulating knowledge to generation after generation. These are our survival skills.

Human adaptation almost always must include adjustment to the social environment as well as the natural environment, that is, to the nearby presence of other groups of humans. We therefore developed the arts of war and diplomacy as well as food production, and these arts inform much of human history.

The idea of cultural adaptation has both positive and negative aspects. On the negative side, we cannot explain all human behavior as adaptive because successful adaptations of culture as a whole include behavior that might be maladaptive, or even irrelevant. No group, for example, eats everything possible in its environment; beliefs and values may rule out certain varieties of edible plants and animals. Some seemingly useless practices continue because they are connected to other practices that are more central and adaptive. Still other practices might continue for reasons of valued tradition rather than for any practical survival value. In other words, cultures do not have to be perfectly adapted to survive.

On the positive side, cultural adaptation requires us to look at a culture in terms of a people's perceived needs and real-life problems in a particular context. The *adaptive focus* of a culture organizes a wide range of behavior and values toward achieving survival goals, as we shall see in a moment. In this view, behavior has purpose instead of seeming to be a chance accumulation of isolated, aimless, and exotic actions persisting out of ignorance and tradition.

Early humans were nomadic, wandering from place to place as they foraged for seasonal food or searched for game. As we spread throughout the world from Africa to Europe and Asia, to Australia by 40,000 years ago, and to North America by perhaps 20,000 years ago, new environments challenged us. Like different languages branching and rebranching from a common linguistic trunk, cultures began to branch into different traditions. The archaeological record shows clearly that we were becoming more efficient and specialized as a result of successfully occupying a variety of habitats. Humans were perfecting arts of survival. With the domestication of plants and animals some 10,000 years ago, some groups abandoned their nomadic life to tend their crops and herds. They lived a new, sedentary way of life. By this time the cultural tree was richly branched; diversity was well developed as different customs, beliefs, and values accompanied technological change in different environments. The common ground was already difficult to find.

Our main problem is to try to understand behavior that we at first do not understand by placing that behavior squarely in the context of real-life problems facing a certain group of people. Doing so undermines our tendency to make ethnocentric judgments, helps us to understand choices and constraints, and humanizes other people. In short, we need to understand the adaptive focus. Toward this end we examine several cases of people living in poverty but making somewhat different adaptations.

Poverty: African American Inner Cities, 1960s

We are interested in studies of poverty in the 1960s for several reasons. It was a time in which firsthand studies of people in poverty began. These studies used the adaptive focus to show how people met a defined set of challenges, thus making their behavior more understandable to outsiders who tended to stereotype the poor as lazy, immoral, and incompetent. Unfortunately, the problem of poverty has not left us today, and some of the same stereotypes and misconceptions of the 1960s persist.

The 1960s was a time of great social upheaval in the United States, a time of inner-city riots, burning ghettos, and racial protests. A stunned and puzzled public witnessed this stormy period and began to ask questions about causes and solutions Although the unrest was answered by rather specific governmental "solutions" focused on restoring inner-city African American families, the mainstream public clearly did not understand what living in poverty was like, and they held many misconceptions and moralistic attitudes about behavior in the slums, regardless of race and ethnicity.

Academic knowledge of poverty was at this time based on second-hand social statistics gathered from census data, social service agencies, and courts and police—traditional information-gathering methods that Charles Valentine (1968:22) exposed as grossly inadequate. With reference to one such work, he observes, "The reader does not get the feeling that the author has observed the life of slum dwellers intensively at firsthand much less participated in that life" (p. 23). Data collected for administrative, rather than scientific, reasons were interpreted by those who had no intensive and prolonged experience in the context in which the data were collected. As Valentine feared, this tradition found its way ultimately into misdirected federal policies, largely in the form of the Great Society program of the Johnson administration.

A second line of thought emerging in the 1960s had at least the value of being based on firsthand observation and participation. The "culture of poverty" described people in poverty living an isolated, self-perpetuating life of violence, crime, alcoholism, and immediate gratification, among other behaviors considered deviant. This idea was elaborated by Oscar Lewis in his work with Mexican and Puerto Rican families (1959, 1961, 1966). The "culture of poverty" is conceived as a subculture that exists in any class-stratified, capitalist society, and therefore is not unique to the United States. The ultimate cause is the larger national and international economic and political constraints that actually set in motion the culture of poverty itself. The immediate cause of the behavior of poor people is a lifestyle featuring short-term adaptations to scarcity learned over the generations, "the culture of poverty." Once this cycle settles in, it generates its own momentum that is hard to stop.

Many (Hannerz 1969, Leacock 1971, Valentine 1968) have noted the conceptual and theoretical inconsistencies in Lewis's work. (Unlike those before him, Lewis at least had firsthand contact with the people about whom he wrote.) What most interests us here, however, is not a general theoretical discussion, but how specific studies done in that era helped us to understand behavior as adaptive to poverty.

Eliot Liebow (1967) studied a small group of street-corner men in Washington, D.C. in the early 1960s. Although he focused on their street-corner activity he came to know them well and to know their social networks. He was particularly interested in their work experience. In one simple but highly effective passage, Liebow describes a scene that an outsider would find difficult to interpret accurately.

> A pickup truck drives slowly down the street. The truck stops abreast of a man sitting on a cast-iron porch and the white driver calls out, asking if the man wants a day's work. The man shakes his head and the truck moves on up the block, stopping again whenever idling men come within calling distance of the driver. At the Carry-out corner, five men debate the question briefly and shake their heads no to the truck. The truck turns the corner and repeats the same performance up the next street. In the distance, one can see one man, then another, climb into the back of the truck and sit down. In starts and stops, the truck finally disappears.
>
> What have we witnessed here? A labor scavenger rebuffed by his would-be prey? Lazy, irresponsible men turning down an honest day's pay for an honest day's work? Or a more complex phenomenon marking the intersection of economic forces, social values and individual states of mind and body? (Liebow 1967:29–30)

Our response after reading the description of the street-corner scene more than likely matches the truck driver's, which is that the men are too lazy to work. Liebow (1967) goes on to identify the men and the fact that some have already worked all night cleaning places such as banks and office buildings; some will go to work in retail stores in another hour or so; some work Saturdays and take their day off during the week; one is going to the doctor; one must go to court, and so forth. Thus, the interpretation of this scene from the insider's view is quite revealing. They all happen to be out on the street corner talking because they are going or coming on business, or for some other identifiable, justifiable reason. Street talk is a regular part of their lives. Being on the street, apparently doing nothing, and apparently refusing work, gives them a high visibility and makes them prey to biased conclusions on the part of the observer.

On the other hand, the street-corner man knows that the jobs he obtains are low-valued jobs—how could he not? He learns to hold menial tasks in the same contempt as do employers and society at large and has no commitment to them. He knows he is expendable, and low pay guarantees his knowledge of this (Liebow 1967:212). These men learn to fail each day, in the present, not as a response to a persisting culture of poverty. Jobs are scarce and low paying, and these workers' racial identity places a ceiling on opportunity and limits choice. These men also fail at their marriages, often blaming their own inadequacies and unwillingness to adjust their behavior. They fail because they cannot economically support a family. They fail because they are trying to achieve many of the values and goals of mainstream culture, but lack the tools and means by which to accomplish their goals. When they fail, they try to hide their failure by rationalizing away their wish for a mainstream life (p. 222). Father and son fail independently because of the present, not because failure is handed down through the generations in a cycle of poverty.

Ulf Hannerz's *Soulside* (1969) is more of a community study in that it describes a variety of lifestyles, including mainstream and street-corner men, and expressive behaviors in a community context. Hannerz also criticizes the idea of a "culture of poverty," although he too sees elements of it being difficult to dismiss entirely. Children do grow up learning some behavior that is at odds with mainstream culture, that is self-destructive or antisocial, but this outcome is neither inevitable nor irreversible. All cultures and subcultures contain maladaptive and self-destructive behavior; for example, in the United States consumerism is ecologically irrational. In the future, such behavior might threaten our survival.

Hannerz (1969) describes people who save, people who spend on personal expressive style, intact families, broken families, and street-corner men. People often express mainstream values although they don't always live them and instead sometimes indulge in "ghetto-specific" behavior (pp. 37–38). This fact does not separate them necessarily from mainstreamers who also do not always act in a manner consistent with espoused values. Anthropologists have come to expect discrepancies between ideal culture and actual behavior. However, Hannerz cautions against building a trait list of behavior that is either ghetto-specific or mainstream because the two categories are ends of a "complex continuum." Particularly, he suggests that it is inaccurate to isolate these behaviors from each other and from the larger culture because they are all relevant to each other and to situations. Both types of behaviors are found in the same person and the same families at different times. Like Liebow, Hannerz underscores the economic weakness of the men as a major problem in maintaining mainstream lifestyles (pp. 74–75).

Liebow and Hannerz provide the reader with extended commentary on the conditions of their fieldwork and their methodology. They exposed some popular myths about work, failure, and families in inner cities, and connected inner cities empirically and conceptually to mainstream culture. They gave us additional insights into the full complexity of poverty and suggested different interpretations of observed behavior.

Poverty: Urban Italy

From another time and another culture, Thomas Belmonte writes a vivid description of adaptation to poverty made by poor families in the slums of Naples, Italy. Belmonte (1989:104) depicts life there as centered on what he calls the "triumvirate of want," love, food, and money. These are the goals, in the context of poverty and violence, which generate the behavior and values of the residents; these goals define their adaptive focus. Children are treated with a mixture of love and violence so that they do not grow up too soft, or too trusting. People practice *impression management* in order to conceal motives and to protect fragile egos. Individual survival requires maneuvering for emotional advantage and the use of physical brutality.

Most households rely on a variety of income sources, both legal and illegal. Those who bring in cash on a regular basis remain integral members, but those who are older and fail to meet this expectation are in jeopardy of being asked to leave. The Neapolitan poor crave money because they don't have it, not because they want to display wealth as do the middle and upper classes. The money is for the present, for survival (Belmonte 1989:104). While this may seem obvious when stated, some of its ramifications for understanding observed behavior are not necessarily appreciated until seen from the inside.

> Being broke is an intolerable condition, analogous to sensory deprivation. It makes a man turn away from his children. It cuts him off from the good company of his friends. He cannot give, and is ashamed to take what is offered. Should he take then what is not offered? The inability to buy a caffe for oneself or to offer it to someone else can set a fire of bitterness growing within a man forcing him to choices and decisions which may alter irrevocably his image of himself and the world. (Belmonte 1989:104)

The personal costs to the individual are high as poverty weighs heavily on his relationships because of his distrust and conflicted identity.

One area where he can exercise some control in his life is impression management, including the display of emotions and personal style of dress. Here he stage-manages his public self for protection and interpersonal maneuvering.

> Perhaps this was why style was so important with the young men of Fontana del Re. For all their swagger, they yearned for accep-

tance by a society that had given them the snub. Style was something that they could appropriate and elaborate upon. Unlike
literacy and salable skills, it was a manipulative part of social identity. Indeed, many of them risk imprisonment to dress well, not to
eat. (Belmonte 1989:132)

Outsiders often misunderstand the reason for style expression, suggesting that if people are that poor they should not be spending their
money on such frivolous things as fancy clothes. However, not spending
on style does not guarantee that they have money to save; it would be
spent alternatively on food, although they often go without meals in
order to purchase "frivolous" things. Individuals need also to feed some
basic psychological needs. Rather than being a failure of character in
the face of hardship, style choice reinforces a fragile young identity
against a brutal world. It is another less obvious ramification of the
craving for money.

Poverty: The Santa Clara Canning Industry

A case study of the canning industry in Santa Clara, California,
gives us an extended and contrasting example of adaptation to poverty
while at the same time it serves as a preview to discussions of culture as
meaning and culture as system (the next two sections of this chapter).

After World War II, the Mexican American population in Santa
Clara jumped from 35,306 in 1950 to 226,611 in 1970 (Zavella 1987:49),
partly because Chicana women quit their migrant labor jobs and
moved to the city to work in the canneries. The major attraction was
that working three to six months a year in the canneries (compared
with working the whole year in the fields) could increase their household income for the year by between one-third and one-half. This
change allowed the family to abandon the migrant labor routes and
remain in permanent residence. The women could also spend six
months or more as traditional housewives, a role many valued. Even
when working, the cannery job afforded a woman a good opportunity to
adjust her shift to complement her husband's work schedule, and such
arrangements reduced their need, in the early stages of the family
cycle, to find babysitters.

Patricia Zavella (1987) studied Chicana women in their dual roles
of traditional housewives and modern cannery workers. She sees her
study as balancing the general view (to be presented later in this chapter) that economic expansion and increased employment opportunity
necessarily open up avenues of job mobility for North American
women. Zavella argues "that the structural constraints on women's
lives and the ideology of family reinforce Chicana subordination.
Within this context, women construct varied meanings of work and
family" (1987:131). By structural constraints, she means historical and
economic setting, labor union competition for representation in the

canneries, and the organization of work at the factories. The cannery labor market passed from craft production to factory system by 1937, through expansion and mechanization by 1968, and reached new levels of production and sophistication by 1978, and thereafter declined. During the middle period, the teamsters won representation, and the labor market segregated into a primary force for men and a secondary force for women. The early mechanization of men's work led to a job hierarchy, a promotion ladder, and hourly wages, while women's work remained ladderless at piece-rates (pay per finished piece) even if their job happened to be mechanized.

The constraints of the work structure and the labor market were not the only problems the women encountered. The traditional conception of the family was that men work and support families and women take care of home and children. Men's wages were usually higher than women's. Yet men were employed in low-paying jobs that were often unstable, thus undermining the basis for the ideal family. Consequently, women often had to find some way to secure additional income. Initially, husbands saw a working wife as a negative statement about their ability to support their family, and as having gained power in the domestic sphere. Later, husbands may have changed their minds as they became accustomed to the extra income. Women also gained some personal satisfaction, some independence, and enjoyed camaraderie with other women in the workplace.

The decision to work usually was made in a discussion with the husband, who probably resisted at first and then "gave in" after the wife went to work. Later, husband and wife negotiated additional understandings. Men were concerned about their personal needs not being adequately served, and both husband and wife were concerned about household operation and child care.

In the later stages of the domestic cycle, with children on their own, women's income became more discretionary and was used for home improvements, new appliances, vacations, or a college education for children. A number of families bought rental properties as a form of capital investment. Women continued to enjoy camaraderie with other women at work, which did not interfere with home and family so that home and work remained segregated from each other.

The women attempted to give meaning to their work by developing a work culture. "Workers use work culture to guide and interpret social relations on the job" (Zavella 1987:100). But they also had to develop the meaning of their work in the context of the traditional family, adjusting the traditional patriarchal ideology. "The meaning women ascribed to their situation as working mothers included acceptance of their primary responsibilities as housekeepers and the need to adapt to the disruption of work" (Zavella 1987:133). The traditional ideology thus became more flexible in the eyes of men and women. Later, when there was less need for income, women still employed the ideology of the traditional family to justify the more personal desires to work. These two meaning contexts contrast with each other but obviously also complement each other.

From the Chicanas' point of view, their adaptation to poverty was the best solution for them at the time. But there was a cost to their decision to complement their family responsibilities, because part-time work reinforced their segregation at work and restricted their job mobility (Zavella 1987:98). On the other hand, they did not have many options, and any job they took would have been a dead end. Almost every form of cultural adaptation is imperfect, requiring trade-offs among several factors important to the participant. In this case they were "optimizing" rather than maximizing their adaptation; they made the best decision for them given the variables important to them.

The number of canneries in Santa Clara fell from a high of fifty-eight in 1930 to eleven in 1982, having been replaced increasingly by electronics firms. Of Zavella's original twenty-four informants, only five were still employed in canneries at the time of her writing. Most had retired. High wages and a shrinking market as U.S. consumers shifted to fresh fruits and vegetables sealed the fate of most of the industry.

The Santa Clara canning industry moved generally in tandem with North American industry, as part of a larger historical stream of industrial maturation and decline, where workers were replaced by high-tech equipment. Mexican Americans, of course, had no control over these events, were poorly prepared for change, and thus could only adapt as they saw best.

No one can read this case study and believe that these women and men are lazy, lack intelligence, are driven by rigid tradition, or fail to use their income effectively—all stereotyped behaviors often erroneously attributed to the poor and minorities. If some Mexican Americans are working in canneries, and if some are working as migrant laborers and others at other jobs, what do these different adaptations tell us about minority stereotyping? Joan Moore (1976:1) observes that "the American-Mexican population probably is more diverse in social composition than any immigrant minority in American history. . . . Therefore, no minority group less deserves simple stereotyping. . . ."

Moore demonstrated, more than a quarter-century ago, the developing internal diversities among Mexican immigrants as they adapt to different historical, political, and economic circumstances in each of the border states where they live in large numbers. Indeed, the umbrella term, Hispanic American, conceals as well the different experiences of Mexican Americans, Cubans, and Puerto Ricans.

The notion of adaptation forces us to see behavior in its context, and from the viewpoint of the insiders. It helps us to see cultures and subcultures in dynamic relationships to the constraints and opportunities in their natural and social environment. This approach can be applied both to other cultures and to intracultural variation, such as perceived race, class, gender, and ethnicity.

CULTURE AS MEANING

The practical arts of surviving and striving are always accompanied by beliefs and values regarding their worth and their place in the world. In the words of Dorothy Lee ([1959] 1987:1–2): "The breaking of soil in the agricultural process may be an act of violence, of personal aggression, of mastery, of exploitation, or self-fulfillment; or it may be an act of worship, and the earth an altar."

The widespread practice of farming is given local meaning. The meaning given is related to the historical traditions of the group and the larger cultural system in which it exists. One might, of course, argue that the essential meaning is clear: we need food to survive. But humans are never satisfied with such a utilitarian explanation, as Lee ([1959] 1987) notes, unless starvation is imminent. We are driven by our very nature to find meaning in our lives. To assign meaning to acts and events is to *interpret* them, to discover their *relevance* and therefore their *consequences* for us. To find meaning prompts us to form an *attitude* toward acts and events. Chicana women did not just work; they had to create for themselves the meaning of their work and their departure from tradition. Street-corner men knew the meaning of their menial work, and they knew its meaning in their lives, although they attempted to deny it. Style choice meant something different to young men in a ghetto of Naples than it did to outsiders.

Specific meanings are characteristically bundled into larger systems of meaning as part of a group's general emotional and intellectual outlook on the world around them. Here, we are interested particularly in the social, the public and shared, aspects of meaning, not in personal meanings and symbols, which would take us into the realm of individual psychology.

Meaning: Sensory Experience

The peoples who anthropologists study, including ghetto residents, often invite us to learn how to see, how to think, and even how to hear their way (Stoller 1989:121). In his *The Taste of Ethnographic Things*, Paul Stoller (1989:5) notes: "This fundamental rule in epistemological humility taught me that taste, smell, and hearing are often more important for the Songhay than sight, the privileged sense of the West. In Songhay one can taste kinship, smell witches, and hear ancestors."

To understand how the Songhay of Niger (Africa) organize and give meaning to sensory experience, Stoller also had to appreciate how the senses have been handled historically in the West, the basis for his own meaning system. The key to sensory meaning in the West is found in the rise of Western science, which is based on visual observation. Thus, seeing, rather than smelling, hearing, or touching, has emerged as the most important sensory experience. We *peer* through microscopes, *read* various scientific instruments, and *observe* subjects. His complaint about most scientific ethnography is that it may be too abstract and too far removed from actual experience, missing therefore the other sensory realities of daily life. Stoller wishes to peel back one more layer of ethnocentrism by inquiring into Western handling of sensory experience through knowledge of other traditions.

Stoller is able to show how the Songhay's speech about their sensory experience is inextricably linked with social relationships. Sight, sound, and taste are organized by Songhay so that everything, from sauces to space, from name-praising to drumming, is given shared meaning. Sauces are good, bad, tasty, or bland according to situations and social relationships. They tend to be prepared best when Europeans visit (1989:16), although the staples are the same. When angry or upset with someone, a bad sauce makes the point. Stoller and his associate were served a meal with an excellent sauce. The cook returned later, clearly wanting to receive something from Stoller. At the next meal, he and his associate received a truly tasteless sauce because the cook was not happy with a black shawl his associate had purchased for her (1989:18–22). The same treatment could be extended to relatives—the quality of sauce being dependent on the current state of a relationship.

In his study of sounds as symbols in a Kaluli system of meaning, Steven Feld (1982), an ethnographer and jazz musician, focuses on songs, poetry, and natural sounds in the environment—especially birds—as these relate to Kaluli (Papua, New Guinea) culture. The Kaluli conceive these sounds as important parts of their emotional style and their social structure; meaning is merged with emotions and social relationships.

> As I wandered among the Kaluli, I began to find a pattern that connected myths, birds, weeping, poetics, song, sadness, death dance, waterfalls, taboos, sorrow, maleness and femaleness, children, food, sharing, obligation, performance and evocation. As I continued to work through the materials, the pattern kept pointing to linkages between sounds, both human and natural, and sentiments, social ethos and emotion. (Feld 1982:14)

The key to understanding connections among those elements mentioned by Feld is the central myth of becoming a bird, the key metaphor for all of Kaluli aesthetics. The Kaluli categorize birds in terms of their physical appearance and the type of sound they emit. The use of songful weeping by women at funerals is considered to be the closest to being a bird; hence a gender variable is introduced. The act of keening relates grief to the myth of the boy who became a bird. As Feld puts it: "weeping moves women to song, and song moves men to tears" (1982:17).

The Kaluli talk about birds in many ways. They use poetic devices to involve audiences and to make them weep. Poetry is thought by the Kaluli to be "bird sound words" (Feld 1982:133). The Kaluli use nature and poetry to speak about their own experience in an emotionally powerful and integrative way. The symbolic merging of nature and culture in native systems of meaning is an integral part of adaptation among many indigenous peoples.

The Kaluli and Songhay examples represent what Hanson (1975:17) calls *implicational meaning*, a meaning assigned to insider behavior by outsiders. "Every cultural thing, like the Rapan prohibition against drinking cold water when hot and perspiring, is linked by implication to other cultural things, like a general hot-cold theory of health and disease, and therein lies its meaning" (p. 10). He sees culture as a logical system, a patterned whole consisting of integral parts. Avoiding a cold drink is linked to a system of beliefs about illness, its causes and cures. So some meaning derives from other, associated meanings, as a part of a coherent system.

The Kaluli know nothing about implicational meaning, which is a social science concept. They are not concerned with whether or not they are acting adaptively, meaningfully, or systemically, which are the descriptive and explanatory inventions of social science; they simply do what they do for reasons that are good and sufficient for them. The Kaluli are but one case among many that anthropologists compile in a strategy of cross-cultural comparison based in part on these concepts. The scientific meaning of acts and beliefs, which is likely part of a Western observer's background, thus overlays local meaning, hopefully without violating its integrity. Any successful ethnography represents a balancing act between building comparative scientific knowledge and accurately reporting the local case.

Intracultural Meanings

The subject of meaning has a political side to it. The meaning of poverty is not the same for mainstream North Americans and poor people. The meaning of race or gender is different for different groups. Mainstream North Americans will see the American flag as a symbol of freedom and opportunity, while some minority groups may see it as a symbol of oppression. Mainstream North Americans and American Indians interpret differently Columbus' "discovery" of the New World. Culture contains both shared and contested meanings. Like other aspects of culture, meaning does not exist in a vacuum, but is firmly located in specific historical contexts—sensitive to the influence of power and wealth.

CULTURE AS SYSTEM

It is important to view behavior as part of a system. Most individual behavior is an expression of a cultural system of beliefs and norms, individuals acting as social persons. Individuals enact, however imperfectly, culturally defined roles and statuses. Roles and statuses are parts of institutions. Economic, political, family, and religious institutions are all part of a larger system. Textbooks in social science treat them individually in separate chapters, but this type of treatment is a pedagogical strategy, not an accurate reflection of reality—in reality, they overlap. As institutions and practices are part of a cultural system, cultures themselves are parts of a larger system, at both national and international levels. All levels and system components are subject to historical influences. The essence of systems is the interrelationships among their component parts so that a change in one produces change in other parts. Constructing the interstate highway system generated profound changes in North American life beyond the simple convenience of efficient travel, by dictating shopping patterns, encouraging suburban growth, and undermining public transportation. The decline of the canneries and subsequent gender role changes were tied to a changing national industrial profile in the post–World War II era.

Cultural systems, however, are imperfect systems containing contradictions and inconsistencies, and are usually undergoing some change. They are sufficiently efficient, but not perfectly efficient. We might regard different systems as natural experiments, with some being more successful than others. Some flourish under change, some disintegrate, some manage to adjust enough to continue. Most sociocultural systems experience more change in some of their institutions than in others. Some parts might lag behind or even resist change.

The adaptive focus stresses *external* relationships, while the systems view stresses the *internal* organization of culture. In stressing the internal aspects of a culture, we run the risk of isolating it from its context. It is easy to see that both views are needed. All cultures today are enmeshed in a web of worldwide relationships of which they are parts. Cultural systems are not isolated, and therefore they are affected by changing contexts and outside influences, which is what makes them so interesting. Cultural systems are *open systems*.

Oscar Lewis thought that he saw a continuing set of relationships among certain behaviors that was a response to the conditions of poverty. He saw poverty as a closed subsystem or subculture that, while set in motion by larger historical circumstances, persisted on its own—the culture of poverty. He was not entirely correct, nor was he entirely wrong. What he did see correctly was a set of related behaviors that might be adaptive in the short run yet maladaptive in the long run, but he failed to stress sufficiently the fact that the culture of poverty, to the extent that it exists, is an open system. In other words, it is susceptible to *ongoing*, contemporary economic and political pressures. There is no inevitable, learned cycle of failure. Rather, contemporary social and economic forces that continue to envelope it better explain the persistence of certain behavior. The case studies in the following sections illustrate interrelationships among different systems levels.

Gender Roles

We will introduce a number of system variables influencing gender definition and gender stratification: (1) the economy and labor market, (2) modes of food production influencing rules of residence and descent, (3) warfare favoring patrilocality, (4) relative income contribution between males and females, (5) degree of segregation between public and domestic spheres, and (6) level of sociocultural complexity.

Gender role definition, and consequently gender stratification, is sensitive to changes in cultural systems. Degree of sociocultural complexity is one important variable in gender definition. In *hunter-gatherer* groups—small, nomadic bands—the relationship between men and women is basically egalitarian (although not completely). Indeed, Patricia Draper (1975) shows gender roles to be interdependent and exchangeable among the traditional !Kung Bushmen. This finding is not surprising for a small face-to-face group where men and women are not heavily burdened with work. But when some !Kung became sedentary, gender separation developed more strongly as men traveled more in search for work by which to acquire cash.

Peggy Sanday (1981) found that where men contributed significantly more income/food in hunter-gatherer groups, gender separation emerged. The same thing happened when women made either a great deal more or less than men. Where men and women contributed about the same, they remained on an equal basis. Thus, even at the hunter-gatherer level, gender stratification begins when incomes of men and women begin to diverge greatly in response to changing local socioeconomic conditions.

At the next level of population size and sociocultural complexity, *rank societies* (horticulturists and pastoralists who produce more food), ideas of biological descent, and rules of residence introduce still other variables. In *patrilineal* societies where descent is traced through the male line, men's public power and authority are supported by descent principles. Usually this type of descent includes the rule of *patrilocal* residence, where the married woman must move to the place of her husband. Removed from many of their kin, women have less support than they would have if they lived in their home community. In a matrilineal society, descent is traced through the female line, and there is an *avunculocal* residence rule where a newly married couple moves to the wife's eldest brother's place. She is still with kin who support her stronger role, although her eldest brother retains public power and authority. The woman is not elevated to a dominant role but does move closer to an equal partnership in many avunculocal descent groups.

Rules of residence and descent are influenced heavily by modes of food production. A change in the circumstances of food production can cause a change in these rules. In their effort to increase manioc flour production for rubber tappers in the Amazon Basin, the Mundurucu changed from patrilocal to matrilocal residence pattern so that mothers and sisters could work more productively.

Rank societies are much more prone to warfare than hunter-gatherer groups, and thus men are more highly valued as warriors. Women, on the other hand, become more important as food producers. Gender stratification is very clear. Kay Martin and Barbara Voorhies (1975) discovered that in a sample of over 500 such societies, over 50 percent showed women doing most of the cultivating, while women and men cultivated about equal amounts of time in 33 percent. Men worked in the fields more in 17 percent of the sample.

Maxine Margolis (2000) documented shifts in attitudes toward women in the United States as the economy and labor needs of the nation changed. Attitudes toward working women relaxed, for example, during World War II when women were required to enter the labor market in great numbers as men were sent off to war. After the war, the attitudes about women in the workforce began to harden again as men returned from service looking for work. However, continuing industrial expansion after the war did accommodate many women who wished to continue working as well as accepting new female workers. Expansion of the economy provided an avenue for women to make good on their political protests in contrast to the early part of the century when opportunities to do so were severely limited.

Against this trend today is the large number of women in poverty, or in transitional states on welfare, because of divorce, loss of husband, or other factors. Also, women tend to occupy lower-paying jobs, and even where opportunities for advancement exist, obstacles on the rungs of the promotion ladder may impede their progress.

Attitudes and definitions often flow from changes occurring in a system. When there are changes in role definitions, whether gender based or otherwise, people reflect on, or give meaning to, what is happening. Zavella's report on cannery workers serves as an example. Remembering that a society can be seen in terms of a role system, we can see that changes in the definition of one role necessitates change in others. The husbands of the Chicana cannery workers were challenged to rethink their own traditional role, regardless of whether they actually changed their attitudes or behavior.

Ethnicity

The studies by Zavella and Moore cited earlier show us how Mexican and Hispanic-American groups must adapt to different socioeconomic contexts in the Southwest, West Coast, and other urban areas of the United States. Cuban immigrants to Florida, who were predominantly middle class and particularly well educated, were well received by the United States as they fled the Castro revolution in the 1960s. It should surprise us little that they have done so well. Other Hispanic-American groups have had varying degrees of preparation, opportunity, and success in other parts of the country. Although they are often stereotyped as a uniform group with an "essential identity," that is, as having some sort of internal quality that marks them no matter what country or time they come from, what actually defines them more sharply is their *relationship* to historical, social, and economic circumstances.

In his *Ethnic Groups and Boundaries* ([1969] 1998), Fredrik Barth notes that ethnicity and ethnic identification are historically shaped and stand in dynamic relationship to the encompassing social system. According to Barth, we should shift our attention from specific tradition and particular beliefs—the internal stuff of ethnic identity, or an essentialist definition—to external relationships. Rather than centering on culture content, we should ask what causes ethnicity to emerge (Barth 1969:17). This perspective allows us to see that ethnicity is more about power, wealth, and competition than it is about traditional ethnic essence. This point needs further illumination.

There is a great tendency to see groups of people in terms of their differences from us. They look different, act different, speak a different language. When they say and do things that we do not like, we attribute it to who they are—to the idea that they are different in an essential way. And while we cannot completely dismiss the influence tradition has on fostering differences, Barth is trying to get us to look past the simple fact of difference and instead focus on the relationships among groups as being more important to understanding ethnic group dynamics. Why is it, he would ask, that tensions between groups rise and fall while the cultural difference between them remains the same? That is, their ethnic essentialism has not changed. What has changed in most cases is their relationship to power, wealth, or territory and thus to other groups. The fact of difference too easily and deceptively becomes the rationale for prejudice and discrimination and the cause of trouble. It causes us to look in the wrong place for sources of friction. An open systems approach offers insights into ethnic group dynamics.

In times of economic hardship and competition, ethnicity is accentuated and the boundaries between groups hardened, while in good times with reduced competition boundaries are relaxed. If each group occupies a different economic niche, as often happened in our early history (one immigrant group dominates laundries, another restaurants, another migrant labor), the situation might be less contentious, but not necessarily.

As Barth (1969:27) notes, interdependence depends on *complementarity* not competition, on stability not change. In direct competition, on the other hand, one ethnic group might displace another, but both stand to lose something because of the potential hostility and conflict between them. For example, the violent acts of skinheads against immigrant laborers in Germany in the 1990s rose in response to the nation's merging of East Germany with West Germany, suddenly creating an excess labor market at a time of economic recession. The two groups perceived that they were in direct conflict with each other. In this context, the ethnicity of immigrants emerged as a salient issue for some Germans, and boundaries tightened. In Northern Ireland, religious difference is only a superficial difference (Darby 1976). The violence is not really over religious dogma, but over political and economic dominance and artificially drawn boundaries. The same is true in the former Yugoslavia, where ancient differences and misdeeds emerged when the Soviet Union departed, leaving a power vacuum. A troubled past is used by present leaders to justify violent acts (Butler 1992). Both Israelis and Palestinians appeal to ancient history and religious doctrine to justify their contemporary claims on territory. Because they are used for present purposes, these past experiences are open to distortion, half-truths, and stereotyping in order to heighten emotions and to increase social solidarity within a group.

Barth's perspective furnishes us with a key by which to understand that ethnicity is not just a matter of cultural heritage but is a dynamic reality in the contemporary world (Middleton 1981). The content of an ethnic culture may remain the same through generations, but ethnic conflict occurs typically in the context of shorter-term economic and political competition as shown above. Clearly, anger and violence can erupt out of simple ignorance and prejudice, but it is the use of perceived difference in a particular competitive context to justify acts against others that most interests social scientists.

Applied Anthropology

At this point, we need to pause to consider the possible uses of our developing understanding of cultural diversity. In what ways could such knowledge be used in a more direct way than just as an informative academic background? Increasingly through the decades anthropologists have been employed either to acquire knowledge of a group for policy implications or to participate in programs of change, and often to do both (Ervin 2005, Gwynne 2003, Van Willigen 2002). We know enough at this point to appreciate how difficult a task either can be.

During the rise of professional anthropology in the late 1800s and early 1900s, anthropologists in North America were hired to enlighten governmental policies used to administer American Indians. British anthropologists were used similarly to inform British colonial administration policies toward indigenous populations. American anthropologists were hired again during the Great Depression, under Roosevelt's New Deal program, and again during World War II to learn more about the enemy. The involvement of anthropologists in the unpopular Vietnam War brought to a head a long-simmering issue about whether or not anthropologists were aiding the government in exploiting native peoples. We will return to this issue in the following chapter. In the 1970s, a series of federal regulations mandated anthropological participation in various federally funded projects, which in effect supported the expansion of applied anthropology as academic jobs became scarce.

The Fox project in the 1940s (Tax 1958) and the Vicos project in the 1950s (Holmberg 1958) are notable early projects led by anthropologists. Sol Tax organized six University of Chicago graduate students to work with a group of Fox Indians in Iowa who lived impoverished lives. The community was encouraged to develop their own projects according to their needs and aspirations, not those of outsiders. Tax sought to combine research with action toward a goal set by the community. Allen Holmberg of Cornell University launched a program of change at Vicos Hacienda in highland Peru. The peasants of the community suffered from poverty and ill health. The project advocated self-help and was successful to the point where the peasants improved their lives sufficiently to buy the hacienda.

Both of these projects encouraged community participation in setting a goal that made sense to them and in developing a means by which to meet the goal. The projects were generally successful for that reason.

Today, many anthropologists are employed in nonacademic jobs, in business, manufacturing, hospitals, and school systems. They do policy analysis, needs assessment, program assessment, social impact assessment, and risk assessment, all in our own culture, as well as in others. In any project, however, practitioners must be aware of the three analytical elements suggested in this chapter.

CONCLUSION

By examining the adaptive, system, and meaning facets of culture we build a suitable framework by which to understand diverse behavior, at least on a preliminary level. By specifying the real-life challenges that a specific group of people face we make sense of their behavior, while preserving their humanity. Seeing different lifeways as related to other lifeways and larger social contexts helps us to avoid isolating people from the forces that impinge on them and influence their behavior. By inquiring into the meaning that people assign to their acts we derive a better appreciation for the human need to make sense of the world and of our place in it. The examples presented in this chapter depict a "lived-in" world of challenges to which people must adapt. If we wish to apply our knowledge to help people we will need to bear in mind the adaptive, system, and meaning perspectives if we are to be successful. The willing participation of the community is critical in any program of change. We are now prepared to examine in more detail some of the problems we can encounter in actually removing prejudice and misunderstanding from our view of the other.

Critical Thinking

1. How are cognitive framework and emotional style related to adaptive focus?

2. Select a current event in the United States or globally and note how different groups involved compete to establish the meaning of the event.

3. Cite several examples of how our culture works as a system of interrelated parts.

Chapter Four

Mirrors and Chasms

When we look at others, we are looking at ourselves, too. We see similarities and we see differences. Comparison is inevitable. We locate ourselves in the sea of human variation by comparing ourselves to others in order to know who we are, or who we are not. Clyde Kluckhohn (1960:16) observed: "The scientist of human affairs needs to know as much about the eye that sees as object seen. Anthropology holds up a great mirror to man, and lets him look at himself in his infinite variety." In this famous passage, Kluckhohn recognizes the comparison that is implicit in our observing others and suggests that we might gain more objectivity about ourselves through an understanding of the sheer variety of cultures that we encounter. In this way we more accurately locate ourselves in the wide range of human variation and achieve a fresh perspective on ourselves. Kluckhohn makes the case that it is easier for the anthropologist to view remote ways of life with detachment and "relative objectivity" (p. 17) because the scene is so different. Kluckhohn focuses on cultural difference.

Kluckhohn's mirror metaphor was useful in helping the public understand what anthropologists of that day were up to and how all people might benefit from their work. However, it does not hold up well in these more contentious times because the mirror is passive, it merely reflects. There is no guarantee that we will recognize the reflected image of ourselves as observers and catch the fresh perspective. Today the "objects," or subjects, seen are not passive but are more vocal about themselves and more critical of the observer than they were in Kluckhohn's day. They want to add to the mirror their own strident voices, their own images. Active engagement of Westerners by others is now a fact of life, an attitude that social scientists are compelled to confront whether or not we wish to. We no longer have a choice. In the past we

67

have too often engaged in a monologue among ourselves about ourselves through others, but now is the time for dialogue. Mirrors, voices, and the eye establish the key metaphors that inform this chapter as we examine our self-critical attempts to understand ourselves and the efforts of the observed to discover their own voices in the modern world. A note on ethics in applied anthropology completes the chapter.

COLONIALISM AND RACISM

Europeans were intellectually unprepared for the discovery of the New World where they found people who not only were unknown but also were not supposed to be there in the first place according to their view of the world. But they were intellectually prepared to accumulate trade goods, precious metals, and gems on which to build the modern European nation, consistent with the economic philosophy of *mercantilism*. European populations were small and spread thinly across the globe. Developing farms, mines, and other projects therefore had to draw substantial amounts of labor from indigenous peoples, most of whom had to be coerced into service by any number of techniques from outright slavery to a tax on their very existence, a "head tax," payable in cash only. Cash could be obtained only by entering the European economic system on its periphery. Native peoples did so at a severe disadvantage because of their lack of knowledge of the system, lack of resources, and paucity of marketable skills. They were nevertheless drawn inexorably into the unending search for cash.

In the context of conquest and colonization there arose a virulent, worldwide assault on the humanity and dignity of humans in the form of *systematic* racism. Prejudice and discrimination certainly existed in the world prior to slavery, and no doubt have been with us since antiquity. The Europeans had expressed racist ideas even among themselves, although not on the basis of skin color, before the existence of slavery. The English brought to the New World particularly rigid ideas about race, which grew out of a folk classification that contained the classic elements of ranked differences, inherited ability, and a close connection between physical characteristics and inner qualities (Smedley 1993). Indeed, they had such ideas about the Irish, whom they utilized in North America as indentured servants. Yet, racism in the context of slavery was a mutant form, new in its widespread and systematic connection to exploiting the labor of people and appropriating their land. As Audrey Smedley points out, the English had very intense feelings about property rights and individualism, which made them protective of their enterprise in slavery, where humans are owned as property.

The technological superiority of the West reinforced its sense of moral and cultural superiority. Communities the world over, suffering from shock, devastated by diseases against which they had no resistance, were dragged into a new culture that they did not understand under terms dictated by dominant Europeans and Americans. Many groups fled momentarily out of harm's way, while others mounted fierce, extended, and frequently effective resistance.

By far, the most devastating technique of control, considered thus because it continues to wreak group and personal damage in myriad ways, was the attack on the psyche of victims through racist ideas. Richard Burkey (1978:95–101) offers a classification of racist ideas employed in controlling people during the initial contact and subsequent colonial periods, which are still with us in one form or another. These are ideal types, of course, and they match reality imperfectly, but nonetheless they give an acceptable overview of racism.

Conflict racism sees subjugated people as treacherous savages, sinister foes, and cunning warriors. They are seen as dangerous and effective in the short run, but no match for advanced cultures in the long run. They lack the qualities of valor and intelligence, not to mention the technology to conduct superior offensive maneuvers. These attitudes were characteristic of many frontiers around the world.

Paternalistic racism is a condescending attitude among politically and economically dominant peoples who see native peoples as charming primitives, happy children, or pathological victims. This pattern of stereotypes persisted in North America until recently as portrayed, for example, in early U.S. movies. No better is the idea that subjugated peoples are more like domesticated animals. Under either misguided belief, native peoples suffered.

THE NOBLE SAVAGE

The Europeans conducted a monologue among themselves about newly discovered peoples in the sense that, while they were eager for new information from the reports of various travelers and explorers, which were often fantastically distorted, they were not seriously interested in what the indigenous peoples had to say about themselves or about Europeans. Hence they did not enter into a productive *dialogue* with them. Instead, various factions of Europeans discoursed with each other about the meaning of the customs and practices of indigenous peoples. Thus, against the *doctrine of degeneration*, which degraded exotic peoples and made Europeans feel better about themselves, European cultural critics used the image of naked innocence, cleanliness, sense of community, and lack of greed reported for many such peoples

to critique moral decline in Europe. They created the image of the
Noble Savage.

While on the surface this idealistic notion would seem to restore
dignity to native peoples, it, in fact, served mostly European interests.
In France, those who had never been near Brazil used the accounts of
Vespucci, the explorer, and others to call for revolutions and independence. Jean Jacques Rousseau, who based his model of the Noble Savage on the Hottentots of southern Africa, but whose ideas of goodness
came directly from Brazilian Indians (Hemming [1978] 1987:23), used
these sources to advance his ideas about the current state of European
political structures. Montaigne, the French political theorist, created a
dialogue in his *des Cannibales* (Hemming [1978] 1987:21) in which he
had the Tupinamba (Brazil) questioning King Charles IX about the
obvious injustices in France. He used the Tupinamba only as political
foils. The Noble Savage distorts the truth as much as degeneration does
by romanticizing native peoples to the other extreme.

The doctrine of degeneration and the idea of the Noble Savage
demonstrate the fact that people try to make sense of differences and
similarities in terms of their own preexisting cultural frameworks.
Information about native peoples was molded to fit European ends.
Few Enlightenment and Renaissance scholars were, in the end, really
prepared to admit savages to the ranks of civilization, equal with themselves. The cultural mirror in this case passively reflected what the
Europeans wanted to see. Native voices were sometimes heard, but not
listened to.

INDIGENOUS RESPONSE AND RESISTANCE

Indigenous peoples and Europeans both were unprepared intellectually for the sudden appearance of equally exotic people. In general,
the Indians of the Brazilian Coast received the explorers peacefully and
with curiosity. They were, of course, fascinated with firearms and with
how metal cut wood, but they were not necessarily appreciative of
strange European values.

The inhabitants of these faraway places also interpreted strange
phenomena based on their own experience and their own way of seeing
things. The inhabitants of Highland New Guinea had never before seen
the imprint of shoes with oddly patterned marks on their soles. These
strange marks suggested to them the foot of a strange and perhaps
frightening skeletal creature who had come from the wrong direction
and walked across the country rather than using the established trails
of the region (Schieffelin and Crittenden 1991:79). What kind of creature was this, they asked? What did it mean? On the other hand, mem-

bers of the Hides expedition into the New Guinea highlands, whose footprints so puzzled the inhabitants, were amazed to observe valleys with farms laid in regular patches reminding them of English farms (p. 110). But how could something so familiar exist in such a primitive place, they wondered (Schieffelin and Crittenden 1991)? Something odd in a familiar place, something familiar in an odd place, both groups struggled to draw meaning from the new experience based on their past experience. Neither was equipped with the experience or intellectual framework to comprehend fully the shock of the new.

Initial contacts between visitors and hosts were often peaceful ones with exchanges of goods and curiosity about each other. The story of American Indians tutoring early settlers on the East Coast in the arts of survival, including how to raise corn, is well known. And, although the explorers were after what they thought were more precious finds, the New World provided settlers eventually with much more valuable materials in the form of corn, cotton, tobacco, chocolate, coffee, potatoes, and sugar. These and other contributions of Indians are often forgotten (Weatherford 1991). Early peaceful relationships did not, however, usually persist. A Tupinamba of Brazil noted to a French Jesuit:

> In the beginning the Portuguese did nothing but trade with us, without wishing to live here in any other way. At that time they freely slept with our daughters, which our women. . . . considered a great honor. But the Europeans invariably began to insist that the Indians help them build settlements, and fortifications to dominate the surrounding country. And, after having worn out the slaves taken as prisoners of war, they wanted to take our children. (Rosenstiel 1983:27)

Eventually, most frontiers involved considerable violence on both parts as Europeans pushed on and native inhabitants defended their land. All over the world Europeans conducted wars of extermination against indigenous peoples. On their part, native peoples resisted, often scoring impressive, if temporary, victories. Plains Indians won a major victory against Custer in the United States in 1876, and the Zulu against the British in Africa in 1879 before being defeated by overwhelming firepower. Other peoples waged long and effective resistance wars against great odds. The Maori wars in New Zealand lasted for twelve years, and Maori courage and skill won the praise of the British troops (Bodley 1990:49).

There were many administrative techniques and ethnocentric justifications for bringing indigenous peoples into the European socioeconomic system. Slavery and the head tax (mentioned earlier) were the more crude varieties. Progress, education, and consumerism were other more powerful ways of enveloping such groups.

To Westerners, then and now, the idea of progress has a magical quality that justifies economic expansion and the culture of consumption, but hides not so obviously a multitude of sins. Those Indigenes who refused, because of their pride in their own way of life, to enter the new system were said to be resisting progress, to be presenting irrational impediments to inevitable change. Cultural practices repugnant to Westerners, such as shamanism and polygyny, and traditional uses of land were obstructions to progress. Land not used for grazing cattle, Western styles of farming, or mining was considered by Westerners to be nonproductive. Native peoples who did not appreciate this fundamental idea were thus refusing (or were unable to understand) to be assimilated into an obviously (in Western eyes) superior culture (Bodley 1990:97–98).

Education in missionary- and government-run schools undermined traditional authority and values and supplanted them with the ways and views of Westerners. Education introduced a new language and new customs while usually denigrating traditional ways. It aimed at nothing less than the transformation of students to the point of assimilation into Western culture, albeit it in an unequal relationship. The lessons of a missionary or government education were more often those of respect, obedience, and politeness than those of fostering intellectual inquiry and an independent spirit (Bodley 1990:103–104). In North America, Indian children were sent to boarding school because it forced their permanent separation from the community (p.104). In this setting, an individual might lose self-esteem as swirling currents of new and old ways buffet him. Education threatens to destroy a traditional sense of self and group membership. Such cultural discontinuities exacted a severe toll on native peoples. On the other hand, a common language, English, would serve later as a basis for pan-tribal unity to confront new challenges.

Consumerism, based on the infinite expansion of markets for manufactured goods, was also an effective way of bringing "primitives" into the fold. A taste for clothing and technology ensured the native quest for cash. An individual would have to enter the system on unequal terms because that was the only way to earn cash. As Bodley points out: "Forced labor, depopulation, reduced land base, loss of traditional food resources, and taxation all helped create a dependency on external goods" (1990:119). Add to these the concerted efforts of governments to introduce superior farming techniques and new or superior livestock, and to convert subsistence land to cash crop enterprises, and a considerable amount of change had already taken place. Education, religion, and consumerism completed the job of conversion to Western ways.

The gains made by Westerners in these faraway places were usually made at the expense of native populations and were instrumented by means of coercion, treaty reversals, and dubious land purchases.

The courts and legislative bodies that legitimized the process of disenfranchisement accomplished much damage. These techniques of control were justified by an underlying Western belief in its own superiority and its mission to civilize the remainder of the world.

IMAGES AND MYTHS

A very large part of understanding bias is to understand that when we appear to be talking about someone else, we are more often talking about ourselves, using the Other to make important points, as did Montaigne and Rousseau. All peoples do the same thing as they interpret events in terms of their own experience and interests. Unfortunately, the historic power differential in favor of Westerners makes their colloquy more consequential for others. In this section, using examples drawn from photography, art, literature, and film, we examine how we perpetuate and disseminate images and myths about other people.

The Power of Images

In their critical study of *National Geographic* (1993), Catherine Lutz and Jane Collins reproduce a photograph from a 1925 issue in which an African porter is pictured peering into a mirror held by a white woman in safari clothes who is laughing and looking at the camera. The caption accompanying the photograph reads "His first mirror: porter's boy seeing himself as others see him," with the authors' additional caption suggesting that this really means that self-awareness comes only with Western contact and technology (p. 210). It is as if there is no other way to self-reflection. Mirrors reflect images, cameras capture them. They both intrude into the lives of others. Power adheres to those who make and dispense mirrors and to those who point the camera and keep the image. In the present example, the idea is that supposedly both camera and mirror evoked in the indigenous person a childish feeling of the miraculous (p. 211). At least, this is the Western imagination.

Photographs of native peoples with mirrors and cameras are a common theme in *National Geographic*, perhaps because for North Americans they are tools for self-awareness. Showing such photographs of them to North Americans resonates on two levels: they are so common in North American life and they play on stereotyping non-Westerners as "childlike and cognitively immature" (Lutz and Collins 1993:207). A camera is both for observation and surveillance as well as for reflection (p. 207), facts that further complicate its use.

National Geographic is the principal purveyor of images drawn from areas outside our border. Established in 1888, it soon became a common feature of middle-class households, which had "aspirations toward the educated, cultured lifestyle of upper middle-class professionals" (Lutz and Collins 1993:17). *National Geographic* tries to adhere to humanistic principles and does not intentionally demean its subjects, which is precisely what makes it a good subject of study. It is not an academic journal, although its status on this score is ambiguous to many of its readers. It is in fact a highly successful commercial operation depending more on not offending readers and giving them what they expect than challenging them. For example, countries out of political favor with the United States get less coverage—none on the former Soviet Union between 1945 and 1959 (although it may have been difficult for outsiders to gain entry) (p. 122). Latin America, particularly Mexico and Central America, received disproportionate coverage (p. 124–125). When China was reopened to the West, eight articles were published in the following ten years. According to their own surveys, *National Geographic*'s articles on Africa are the least popular, and those involving social problems in that area, least of all.

The Pacific is a popular region, and the photographs tend to feature women with bare breasts, often dancing. Men are shown as skillful navigators in traditional canoes. Another common theme is the arrival of the modern world, where, for example, one photo shows an Islander's navigator stick next to a radar screen for maximum contrast antiquated and modern.

The Melanesian Islands, so named because the inhabitants are darker skinned than their neighbors, receive treatment different from other Pacific Islanders, with many photographs showing men peering into mirrors while applying facial paint and other decorations accompanied by captions suggesting pride and primping. These are images and words that draw contrasts between the viewer and those who are shown. Women are frequently depicted as hard working, exotic, or beautiful objects, but primarily aspiring to be like Western women. Black women are treated differently. "The racial distribution of female nudity in the magazine conforms in pernicious ways, to Euroamerican myths about black women's sexuality, lack of modesty in dress places black women closest to nature" (Lutz and Collins 1993:172).

These photographs are not objective records, but instead they mirror for the viewer his own fantasies and unrecognized ignorance of other people, his ethnocentrism. They make the viewer feel better by meeting the viewer's expectations, rather than by challenging them. They do not encourage a self-critical attitude.

The Educated Eye

Primitive art offers a pointed example of how the West appropriates, categorizes, and judges aspects of other cultures. It illustrates how various Western interests converse among themselves about others, instead of with others. As Sally Price puts it, the subject is "those who have defined, developed, and defended the internationalization of Primitive Art, and on their racial, cultural, political, and economic visions" (1989:5).

This is not the place to explore various definitions of primitive art, except to note that we have the usual problem of trying to define an enormously diverse world of objects representing various technological capacities, styles, and interests, too conveniently wrapped in a highly questionable classification. The term obviously carries with it a heavy load of ethnocentric baggage. Our focus, instead, is: how the West has used that material covered by the term, *primitive art*.

The fact that Western self-appointed "experts" imagined more about the wellsprings of primitive art than they knew about the cultures and the artists themselves meant that they could give free rein to their own fantasies and ethnocentrism about the subject. Many connoisseurs seemed to think they had a natural gift for knowing what was good, untainted by their own culture. Somehow, whatever the provenance of an art object, they thought that they had a universally applicable taste for fine art. Price (1989:19) joins other anthropologists (Bourdieu 1984, Sahlins 1985) in noting that there is no eye that has not been educated. The expert eye is still a product of its experience and culture and does not automatically perceive the designs and products of other cultures in unbiased light.

The West creates many myths about primitive artists. One is their childlike quality:

> Just as children cry when they are hungry and coo when they are content, Primitive Artists are imagined to express their feelings free from the intrusive overlay of learned behavior and conscious constraints that mold the work of the Civilized artist. And it is this quality that is most often cited as the catalyst for understanding between Westerners and Primitive artists. (Price 1989:32)

As she further notes, the racist foundation underlying the notion that primitive art is like children's art is rather transparent (p. 32). African art is particularly labeled in such fashion. Blacks are often thought to represent the childhood of humankind—stalled at an earlier stage of development. Again, we find that the dialogue is in one direction only.

> *We* partake of an identification with African art; this allows *our* self-recognition and personal rediscovery and permits a renewed contact with *our* deeper instincts; the result is that *we* increase *our* understanding of *ourselves* and *our* relationship to art. (Price 1989:37) [italics in original]

Price continues with the pithy comment that the Noble Savage and the Pagan Cannibal are the same person "described by a distant Westerner in two different frames of mind" (p. 37). It is not the case, of course, that we should refrain from trying to make sense of primitive art in terms we can relate to our own world—translating culture as we translate languages—but that we should understand our forms of self-deception and ways of maintaining distance.

A series of self-deceptions and misunderstandings mark Western discourse on primitive art. Westerners often characterize Primitive artists as slaves to tradition, fears, spirits, and eroticism because they are close to nature, or undeveloped. It is therefore reasoned that they are probably not making conscious design choices based on clearly articulated aesthetic principles. We tend to locate them in a timeless past, rather than in their struggles with the modern world. Contrasting modern art and primitive art places cultural distance between them and us (p. 63). These beliefs reveal a widespread ignorance of other cultures and dehumanize others as unreflective and unchanging people.

Another critical ingredient in maintaining distance is the fundamental difference in the amount of power that Westerners and primitive artists exercise in the process of art production, distribution, and appreciation. Westerners determine what is good or bad, what is "in" or "out." (Price 1989:68–70). Those who have the power to define and to label do not hesitate to do so. Those on the other end too often begin to conform to the images assigned to them, as when art is made to conform to the outsider expectations of tourists.

When Western art is displayed in a Western museum for a Western audience there is less need for detailed labels describing context, motive, and design, because all elements are from the same cultural tradition, and assumptions can be made about what already is known. But how much should we explain an art display from a tradition different from our own? More enlightened gallery directors today appear to be trying to elevate the status of some primitive art by reducing contextual display and label explanation (Price 1989:82–99), thinking that any viewer will appreciate its intrinsic beauty. It can stand alone. Conversely, too much contextualization throws it back into the category of an ethnographic museum, which does a better job of contextualizing it but perhaps removes it from the realm of art.

It is unlikely that the "primitive" artist will be asked to rule on what is a masterpiece in either culture. But leaving primitive art decontextualized leaves too much room for myths and misunderstandings to operate freely. Contextualization, on the other hand, can re-educate the eye. Because such art is so easily misunderstood, fuller explanation might be the better course, leaving decisions about whether a work should be viewed as art or artifact for later.

Tourist arts (Graburn 1976) offer particularly interesting examples of culture contact and confused perspectives. Australian Aborigines painted their bodies and sometimes the bark of their dwellings in the service of ritual. They did not sell their bark paintings (Williams

1976:271). Missionaries at Yirrkala on the northeast coast of Arnhem Land in Australia introduced to these hunters and gatherers the idea of developing self-sufficiency in a cash economy based on the sale of traditional arts. Missionaries sold the bark paintings to museums and universities, but with the stipulation that all work had to be genuinely traditional with no innovation (p. 274). By 1964, missionaries in the area were issuing certificates of authenticity with sales of Aboriginal artwork (p. 277).

Although there was a strain toward producing artwork that would be aesthetically pleasing to the white buyer (Williams 1976:272)—particularly with respect to its fit and finish—the Aboriginal artists responded, and there seemed to be a restoration of community pride in the fact that outsiders would purchase their art. In fact, what was happening was that contemporary native art was performing a traditional function: "to reinforce and to enhance an important aspect of traditional culture, and the values it expresses" (p. 282). Youths who wanted to be artists had first to learn the traditional lore and values—which stand as law—of the community.

Purists would like to see native art for sale to outsiders certified for authenticity, with no innovation, and untainted by Western values, so that tourists know that they are getting the real thing. Those who hold the opposite view, emphasizing continuing adaptation, would like to see people free to innovate and to draw on their traditions to sustain them as they make a transition into the modern world. From bark paintings, some Aboriginal artists have moved to acrylic on canvas and combined traditional imagery with new viewpoints to interpret their contemporary circumstances. Both purist and adaptation views surface in the example of Aboriginal art, as well as tourist art in general. Should we keep people poised to produce for museum display, preserving some imagined original state, or permit them to enter the modern world through their art? As Price points out, however, the power differential works against traditional artists in the contemporary world, although some today have works in national museums and fine art galleries. Traditional art is not just traditional, but adaptive at one time to past circumstances that are now changed.

The tension between purist and adaptation views is mirrored in ideas of preservation and conservation. Preservation supports authenticating the past, an attitude that carries with it valuing the traditions of a people whose culture has been denigrated for centuries. This view, however, denies a community the value of continuing to adapt to a changing world. The idea of conservation (Hufford 1994) allows for both tradition and change. The conservation approach permits the local community to adapt its traditional perspectives to its contemporary experience. Tradition in this view becomes a vibrant, living fund of knowledge, rather than a dead museum piece. The art of the Runa

(Ecuador) illustrates the adaptive value of art as well as the value of applied anthropology (Whitten and Whitten 1988). Traditional pottery and carved balsa wood forest creatures both sustain key traditional beliefs and values as well as make statements about contemporary events. Their art also brings in badly needed cash. They feel that they are exercising some control over the pace and direction of change. They are neither passive nor powerless pawns in the modern world, and they have been assisted by outsiders.

The Myth of Africa

Stereotypes of native peoples can be widely disseminated through popular literature. In their study of some five hundred books of fiction and nonfiction on Africa, Dorothy Hammond and Alta Jablow (1977) discovered that the literary image of Africa, beginning with the period of slavery, is a "fantasy of a continent and a people that never were and could never be" (p. 14).

> African behavior, institutions, and character were not merely disparaged but presented as the negation of all human decencies. African religions were vile superstitions; governments but cruel despotism; polygyny was not marriage, but the expression of innate lusts. The shift to such pejorative comment was due in large measure to the effects of the slave trade. A vested interest in the slave trade produced a literature of devaluation, and since the slave trade was under attack, the most derogatory writing about Africans came from its literary defenders. (Hammond and Jablow 1970:23)

In response, the antislavery literary figures set about to create a new Africa based on the idea of the Noble Savage, who was, in this case, the African prince or princess, who looked more European, shared British values, and was representative of royal lines. The real tragedy was that royalty had been reduced to servile status (Hammond and Jablow 1977:27).

Africa became a metaphor for all that was dark, animalistic, and horrific. It stood for the dark interior of the civilized person with whom one had to come to grips. It was a timeless land. Africa tested one's character. Men went to Africa to become men, to maintain their values and their discipline in the face of unimaginable hardship, and to overcome ordeals. Africa serves as a convenient example of ethnocentric projection, but the same themes were common throughout the colonial world.

The modern world continues to have a voracious appetite for similar stereotypes. In 1956, Elizabeth Marshall Thomas wrote a popular book on the San people of southern Africa, entitled *The Harmless People*. The book, buttressed by an educational film, *The Hunters*, educated two generations of college students on the people of this region. The educational film and book depicted the San as both harmless and charming, and living a life that represented an earlier stage of cultural development. Students may well still be receiving that message. In 1981, a film that included the San, *The Gods Must Be Crazy*, became immensely popular throughout the world. It depicted, stereotypically, the San as living in childlike innocence and primitive affluence free of the woes of civilization. Its impact on the San, or Bushmen as they are more popularly known, was disastrous as other film crews descended on them with great regularity (Gordon 1992:1).

Some San live near the Tswana where Marianne Alverson received her lesson in reading the sands (see chapter 1). They have a justified image for being excellent trackers, but their skill, which some outsiders regard as superhuman, is learned, their eye educated. Their skill is not necessarily to be admired because it tends to be closely associated in the minds of outsiders with people of animalistic nature; the myth dictates that only a creature close to nature could be so acutely attuned to its natural environment. The supposed fact that they are "natural trackers" (as opposed to learning to adapt) accentuates their difference from civilized people.

The San have no umbrella name for themselves, but recognize only individual groups. In his study of the "Bushman Myth," Robert Gordon focused on the "the colonizer's image of them and the consequences of that image for people assumed to be Bushmen" (1992:4). Like Africa, the San have been rediscovered by governments, churches, news media, scientists, and laypeople at various times according to their own agendas. Consequently the San have not always been the harmless people. Because of their learned tracking skill, the San were heavily recruited into the South African Defense Force (SADF) during the 1980s to help them fight a guerilla war against the South-West People's Organization (SWAPO), a militant nationalist group (Gordon 1992:2), for which the San were paid. Thus, the San, who had few means of acquiring cash, could use their tracking skills to do so.

Early in the history of contact, they successfully fought against a variety of intruders. Gordon (1992:7) observes that they have "the longest, most valiant, if costly, record of resistance to Colonialism." Indeed, the word, San, proposed by those who believe that "Bushmen" is sexist and racist, more likely means "bandits" (pp. 5–6). It would be an accurate label for their historical and violent struggle on the frontier.

As elsewhere, outsiders draw a contrast between themselves and the San—wild natives against civilized peoples. Untamed or undomesticated, like animals, they are unlikely to be assimilated into civilization. Their distinctiveness has been premised on their different physique (they are small in stature), and different culture and values, and has supplied outsiders with a constant source of myth making for their own purposes. As Gordon (1992:212) points out, these were not descriptive categories, but a principle of colonization. These are not isolated, harmless, backward, or affluent people; they are, in Gordon's terms, people who live in a state of "integrated rural poverty" plagued by illness, hunger and powerlessness (p. 3). They are very much a part of the modern world system and their nation, but they are increasingly becoming a dependent "underclass" in a cash economy.

NATIVE RESURGENCE AND POLITICAL ACTIONS

After World War II, American Indians began to speak strongly and act forcefully to bring public attention to their cause. In the 1960s they staged a "fish-in" in the Pacific Northwest to assert their treaty rights. They seized Alcatraz in 1969, seized the Bureau of Indian Affairs headquarters in 1979, and shortly after they seized Wounded Knee. Wounded Knee is highly symbolic because on December 28, 1890, approximately 100 Sioux warriors and 250 women and children surrendered to the U.S. Seventh Cavalry. They were being moved to a reservation, but twenty miles short of their destination, violence erupted as soldiers searched tents for weapons. Men, women, and children were massacred, with very few escaping (Cornell 1988:3).

These seizures mark some of the important milestones in American Indian efforts to revitalize themselves and their culture and to make their way in a world in which they have had little power. Cornell (1988:8) observed: "Groups act not only *within* limits set by forces beyond their control, including their own distinctive histories. They also act *upon* those limits. In the process they may remake themselves and the world in which they live, and thereby the conditions under which they act." American Indians have been remaking themselves and acting on limits particularly over the past three decades. The stereotypical and dominant treatment of American Indians required a response based on a common, supratribal consciousness (Cornell 1988). Native Americans did not use inclusive terms to describe themselves until it became politically necessary to present a common front. Like the San, they tended to think of themselves as individual groups until political reality forced united action.

In his popular book, *Custer Died for Your Sins* (1969), Vine Deloria, Jr., captured the essence of white–Indian perceptions of each other in clear and simple terms.

> Because the Negro labored, he was considered a draft animal. Because the Indian occupied large areas of land, he was considered a wild animal. (p. 8)

> Whenever Indian land was needed, the whites pictured the tribes as wasteful people who refused to develop their natural resources. Because the Indians did not "use" their lands, argued many land

> promoters, the lands should be taken away and given to people who
> knew what to do with them. (p. 10)

> But Indians have been cursed above all other people in history, In-
> dians have anthropologists. (p. 78)

> It has been said of missionaries that when they arrived they had
> only the Book and we had the land. Now we have the Book and they
> have the land. (p. 79)

Native peoples of South America also have acted decisively to
adapt to their current circumstances while attempting to preserve
their traditional ways as much as possible. In recent years, jarring
images in the popular press of feathered and painted Indians wielding
video cameras have jolted the stereotyped images of non-native view-
ers. One such group, the Kayapo of Brazil, took up the camera partly as
a way of documenting their agreements with national officials and
other parties, such as gold miners, who often reneged on their prom-
ises. They have been skillful users of modern media to gain national
attention and push demands as have others in Amazonia like the
Xavante. Some Kayapo have become accountants in order to keep their
own books on their receipts from gold miners who work on their land,
access to which they tightly control. They take a percentage of the gold
that is shipped out.

The resurgence of native peoples in the Amazon Basin is led by
those groups who have had the longest contact with Westerners, and
therefore more time to recover from the ravages of early contact. These
people never wished to be Western and resisted until their population
recovered and until they learned more of the world that dominated
them. They now see that they must deal, as Cornell said, with the world
as given them, and to remake themselves. This means educating teach-
ers, medical personnel, lawyers, and accountants and honing the skills
to manipulate modern media to their advantage.

Similarly, the Shuar, "headhunters," of Ecuador have teamed with
their other Jivaroan-speaking neighbors to create a *federaccion* that
has become quite successful (Bodley 1990:160–162). They have oper-
ated a radio station since 1968, published a bilingual newspaper, and
produced their own film on their traditional ways. At the same time,
their culture has changed significantly over the years. They believe
that they have generally changed for the better, but more important,
they feel that they control the pace and direction of change.

These groups are now linking up internationally with other
groups in Canada, the Philippines, and Australia. Such groups as
IWGIA (International Work Groups for Indigenous Affairs), World
Council of Indigenous Peoples, Cultural Survival, and Survival International are supported additionally by private persons, churches, and
the United Nations (Bodley 1990:177).

THE ETHICS OF FIELDWORK

Native peoples seek new avenues of expression and support in the world as given. As they do, they become more wary of the uses anthropologists make of the information they collect from them. Some highly publicized ethical issues unfortunately have cast suspicion on some fieldwork. Professional concerns surged during the unpopular and widening Vietnam War. Particularly troubling to many anthropologists was an associated project in Thailand (Van Willigen 2002:50–51). This project was ostensibly a program to compile ethnographical knowledge of the Northern Hill Tribes. A number of anthropologists were funded to do research in the area. However, the project was a poorly veiled counterinsurgency program to compile strategic information on poor and isolated groups who grew opium and were thought to be subversives who might attack the government, as in Vietnam. The collected information eventually ended up in the U.S. Department of Defense. As a result of this revelation, and others, The Society for Applied Anthropology issued a new ethics statement in 1969 (Whiteford and Trotter 2008: 5, 38–41).

Regardless of the ethical dilemmas faced by anthropologists, the field of applied anthropology continues to grow, and native peoples frequently request assistance from fieldworkers. As daunting as the moral challenges noted in chapter 1 are, the applied worker faces even more, and can find herself in no-win situations where different ethical principles clash with each other (Whiteford and Trotter 2008). In Medical Anthropology (Gwynne 2003:247–267) or Business Anthropology (Gwynne 2003:203–221) (Jordan 2003:54–62), the fieldworker is most likely not working for herself, but for an organization. She thus has obligations to the organization as well as to the group she is studying. It is incumbent on the fieldworker to understand the organization for which she works as well as the group she is working with.

Today, there are various professional and institutional guidelines for human research. Basic to all of these standards are three principles: (1) "respect for persons, (2) maximize good for people and minimize harm, and (3) ensure basic justice for people participating in human research" (Whiteford and Trotter 2008:46).

CONCLUSION

We can agree with Kluckhohn that looking at others is like looking into a mirror and getting a fresh view of ourselves, but we should question whether or not the passive mirror metaphor alone is any longer a sufficiently useful one. Adding the voices of others would capture the more strident spirit of today.

The doctrine of racial inferiority accompanied the age of European colonization of most of the world, and it supported a campaign of domination and exploitation. The Europeans had a vested interest in defining and categorizing indigenous peoples. Even the seeming altruistic ideal of the Noble Savage served more the political philosophies of the Europeans regarding the European state than it did those so classified. Native peoples were twice defeated: they everywhere fought and resisted European incursions, but were eventually defeated by force and disease. In the aftermath, the insidious forces of religion, education, and consumerism usually defeated them once more.

Myths about darkest Africa, misunderstandings of primitive art, and the distorted images conveyed to us by popular media tell us more about ourselves than they do about other people. In recent decades, native and minority peoples, formerly relatively voiceless, have found their voices and taken active steps to control their future. The many ethical challenges anthropologists face are compounded when working in applied anthropology, but there are many ethical guidelines available to help the academic fieldworker, and the applied anthropologist.

Critical Thinking

1. Where do your images of other people come from? Books, television, movies, family, friends? To what degree are you aware that your images may be stereotypes?

2. Why is there no such thing as primitive art?

3. What do you think is meant by the phrase, "make the exotic more familiar, and the familiar more exotic"?

Chapter Five

The Comparative Perspective

On April 23, 1991, the largest McDonald's restaurant in the world opened in Beijing. With 700 seats and 29 cash registers, Beijing McDonald's served 40,000 customers on its first day of business. Built on the southern end of Wangfujing Street near Tiananmen Square—the center of all public politics in the People's Republic of China—this restaurant had become an important landmark in Beijing by the summer of 1994, and the image of the Golden Arches appeared frequently on national television programs. It also became an attraction for domestic tourists, as a place where ordinary people could literally taste a bit of American culture. (Yan 1997:39)

McDonald's penetration into China, a communist country often alleged to be an adversary of the West—and at a world-famous site of bloody, youthful resistance to the political system just a few years before—is a dramatic example of the extent to which McDonald's has globalized its operations. Between 1995 and 2000 the number of McDonald's in China increased from 62 to 326 (a 429 percent increase). Globally, it operates about 28,000 restaurants in over 100 countries (The Globalist 2001). This is interesting information, but what has it to do with the comparative perspective in anthropology? The answer to this question is best deferred to the end of the chapter ("Controlled Comparison: McWorld"), after we have laid the proper groundwork for further discussion.

The work of anthropology can be conveniently characterized as a continuing struggle to strike a proper balance between extreme viewpoints on three key questions. The first question asks where is the appropriate point of balance located between the insider view of those who live their culture and the outsider view of those who observe them? The second question asks about the degree to which we should emphasize our common ways on the one hand and our lived differences on the other. We addressed both of these questions in previous chapters. From these questions emerges a closely related third one: how can we move beyond a detailed knowledge of a single culture to a more general understanding of the many without distorting the one? The answer to this question lies in the proper use of the *comparative perspective*.

Striking a proper balance on these questions is like walking an intellectual tightrope because the balance point is always unstable. It is in constant motion because new theoretical views emphasizing one side or the other continually appear. On the question of cultural comparison, anthropology historically has shown a tendency to teeter between cultural uniqueness and cultural comparability. The strong view of uniqueness (extreme cultural relativism) is that if cultures are considered unique, then, by definition, they cannot be compared with each other. This view argues that parts of culture taken out of their context, like words taken out of context, lose some of their original meaning and the comparison is distorted. The weak view recognizes that each culture should be understood on its own terms, especially when working at the level of a detailed descriptive model of one culture, but only up to a point. Proponents of the weak view would argue that no culture is so unique that it is not recognizably human and therefore shares a certain commonality with other cultures. In the weak view, one can, with care, make useful comparisons based on this commonality, while working toward an understanding of both similarities and differences.

How far to go in either direction is an inherently unanswerable question because it is a matter of intellectual choice to emphasize one side or the other. Most anthropologists would take neither extreme view. Indeed, if the discipline shifts too far to one extreme, those who are less extreme in their viewpoint work to nudge it back toward the center. Consequently, the discipline generally has been balanced precariously on this intellectual tightwire for well over a century. Although this uncertainty may be unsettling for some scholars, it is probably the healthiest strategy for anthropology because it keeps in play its self-critical attitude about what it is doing and why.

The fact is that all anthropologists eventually are forced intellectually, as a matter of human curiosity as well as professional interests, to make at least the basic form of comparison: to compare and contrast their study community with their home community. Larger questions of how and why similarities and differences exist between communities inevitably arise and cannot be ignored. Moreover, comparison is bred fundamentally into the discipline, inherent even in the basic work that anthropologists do.

> Comparison is the bread and butter of anthropology. It is inherent in the act of classification, by which we identify unfamiliar behaviors, describe institutions, and communicate the results of our work to others. We cannot describe one society without having others in mind, for comparison is the recurring element in our basic analytical tools. Comparison establishes and refines a common discourse among scholars working with different cultures; it stimulates and provokes new perspectives on findings from particular cultures; and it allows us to search for general principles through controlled comparison. Comparison elevates the level of our work to the quest for principles of human life that transcend any one culture, even as it accepts the importance of culture in forming people's interest and the views they have of others. Without comparison we risk miring our work in exotica and the description of the particular. (Gregor and Tuzin 2001)

Anthropology is the general study of humans in all times and places, not just a study of specific communities and their unique ways of life. These specific communities are living experiments, expressions of common humanity under varying historical, ecological, and cultural circumstances from which spring cultural differences. These natural experiments taken one by one tell us much about human capacity and adaptability, but a single case of keenly observed adaptation cannot alone tell us all we want to know about human life. On the other hand, those who are wary of cross-cultural comparison have good reason to be critical because this perspective holds many intellectual pitfalls as the history of comparative study illustrates.

EARLY COMPARISONS

As the European colonial powers swept inexorably over distant lands in their relentless search for precious metals and natural resources, they encountered a bewildering variety of cultures that challenged their narrow view of the world. By their history and local interests, the Europeans were intellectually unprepared to meet this challenge. What frameworks regarding the peoples of the world were available to them to organize their thoughts about cultural diversity? In what ways did they succeed, or fail, in meeting their challenge?

Degeneration and Progress

The worldview of Medieval and Renaissance Europeans did not allow for the existence of exotic peoples, because the Europeans' experience covered mostly their own region and the Middle East. As various travelers and explorers reported on their foreign ventures, collectors of these descriptions of exotic customs, who were known as *encyclopedists* and *cosmographers,* compiled popular, fantastic, and false accounts of other peoples. Interpretations of the meaning of these curious customs, true of false, were left mostly to the reader. With few exceptions, these and similar works exoticized and, in modern terms, "marginalized" the humanity of newly discovered peoples. Differences were emphasized in comparison with European standards to the extent that perceptions of cultural differences raised questions about whether these people were really human and part of the biblical story of creation. Because Europeans saw these previously unknown peoples as having been isolated from the benefits of Christianity and Western civilization, they came increasingly to see them as degenerate humans to be exploited and as needing the benefits of contact with the Church and "civilization." Decline and degeneration were ideas supported in the minds of adherents by such reported practices as cannibalism, witchcraft, beliefs in ancestral spirits, and strange systems of family and marriage. The *doctrine of degeneration*—combined with materialistic greed, misinformation and misunderstanding, and the need for large pools of inexpensive labor—justified, in the minds of many Europeans, the subjugation of colonized peoples.

The cosmographers were enthralled by diversity, which was the principal criterion for including native peoples in their collections. However, their purpose was to entertain, not to advance a science of culture. The Church, on the other hand, had a vested interest in classifying diverse peoples as heathen. It wanted to save souls and to extend the dominion of the Church. The Church was one of the central connecting threads running through European society over the centuries. It had served the poorly educated public as the principal guardian of morality and key interpreter of worldly experience. But Europe was changing; the voyages of discovery and the work of colonization were both expressions and accelerators of sweeping changes in the social structure of the Medieval period. The Feudal era was ending and the era of modern state formation was beginning and driving the expansion of global trade.

The *Renaissance*, or "rebirth," was a diffuse and ambiguous era that began in Italy and moved northward through Europe in the fifteenth century. More of a "flowering" of the arts than a scientific revolution, the era displayed a robust interest in the human condition in everyday life rather than a preoccupation with heavenly affairs of interest to the Church. The cosmopolitan outlook of Renaissance thinkers delighted in the seemingly endless diversity of other peoples. But as time passed, science was making headway; much discussion began to center on the possibility of discovering natural laws that explained natural events and perhaps human behavior.

Spanning the seventeenth and eighteenth centuries, the *Enlightenment* was an era in which people believed that the world could be *understood* and *controlled* without supernatural (God) assistance but by the principles of reason, that is, by a *naturalistic* approach. Humans were considered to be part of nature, not above it, and therefore obeyed the laws of nature. Following this view, some scholars searched for laws of society that could account for *both* similarities and differences. John Locke (1632–1704), in *An Essay Concerning Human Understanding* ([1690] 1974), expressed his view that humans everywhere are born as "empty cabinets" and become different to the extent that they fill the cabinets with different life experiences. This seems to be an incipient idea of culture—an emphasis on acquired behavior. *Thus, where the Renaissance exalted in diversity as an expression of humanity, the Enlightenment searched for the laws of society that commonly operate beneath the surface differences.* In an abstract sense, Enlightenment scholars such as Locke believed that human nature was everywhere the same, but they also believed that cultures progressed through time and that European culture had clearly progressed the furthest. To admit that native peoples had potential to become civilized did not necessarily mean to these scholars that they were equals. By the nineteenth century, ideas of progress and development were widespread throughout Europe and are an integral part of Western thought today.

Progress and Development

Charles Darwin, in his *The Origin of Species* (1859), reaffirmed with voluminous documentation the Enlightenment's faith in our ability to discover the laws of nature and progress. In his concept of *natural selection,* Darwin made the struggle for survival in nature serve the cause of progress. Progress achieved through natural selection is measured by the successful adaptation of species to environmental conditions, which leads to improved, better adapted forms of creatures in succeeding generations. All of living nature, including humans, is subject to this process. Whereas Enlightenment scholars tended to think that the human species was somehow at the summit of progress, those espousing biological evolution believed there is no ultimate end point; development is an ongoing response to changes in the environment without any goal other than to adapt to the circumstances. As a part of this intellectual movement, a young social science in the 1800s began to think of diverse and exotic peoples as examples, not of how far they had fallen, but of how far Europeans had progressed, as if they were the improved and perhaps final forms of the human species. Cultural evolutionists conveniently ignored the biological evolutionists' denial of an inevitable "end point."

The search for laws of nature and society transformed the old preoccupation with decline into new a commitment to development theory, or cultural evolution. Amateur anthropologists seized on this idea to fashion models of human cultural development based on progressive stages. These progressive models suggest that significant cultural diversity arises from different levels of cultural *development*. The organizing principle in this strategy is a comparative one of sorting different customs and artifacts into categories representing hierarchical stages of development. This approach to cultural comparison is known as *classical evolutionism*.

Edward B. Tylor (1832–1917), an English Quaker, and Lewis Henry Morgan (1818–1881), a lawyer from Rochester, New York, were two of the more astute practitioners of classical evolutionism and are recognized founders of modern anthropology. Indeed, Tylor wrote perhaps the first textbook, *Anthropology* (1881), and included in it archaeology and a rudimentary physical anthropology. Morgan worked with the Iroquois and wrote *Ancient Society* (1877). What interests us most about these scholars is their contribution to organizing cultural diversity by use of comparative methods and the problems they encountered in doing so.

Edward Tylor accepted the idea of human progress through evolutionary stages of culture and focused on the development of different institutions such as religion, law, and descent systems. Tylor believed that human efforts to explain such natural events as death and dreaming by referring to the supernatural led to the birth of religion, a cultural universal. This broad statement includes all religions and facilitated comparison by not getting hung up on a more detailed definition of religion. He proposed that the development of religion progressed from *animism* to *polytheism* to *monotheism*. Tylor, however, noted that the development of religious ideas was much more complex than indicated in a simple three-stage sequence.

In order to reconstruct stages of cultural evolution, Tylor embarked on an enormous amount of comparative work that is reflected in *Primitive Culture* ([1871] 1958). He developed a habit of cross-checking data wherever possible because he knew that some of the data were flawed. Untrained observers with varying degrees of experience, insight, and bias reported them. In an early example of statistical global comparison, his "On a Method of Investigating the Development of Institutions, Applied to the Laws of Marriage and Descent" (1889) drew from reports on nearly 300 societies to establish statistical correlations among cultural traits relating to marriage and descent.

While Tylor and many other evolutionists focused on the development of different institutions like religion, Morgan ([1877] 1963:12) established sequences in which he placed whole cultures. These sequences—savagery, to barbarism, to civilization—were based on increasing technological sophistication.

One of Morgan's most important contributions was his comparative study of kinship. In addition to collecting data for what became his highly respected description of Iroquois matrilineal descent and classificatory naming of relatives ([1851] 1962), he mailed an extensive questionnaire to his contacts abroad asking about native kinship systems (1871). Like Tylor, he believed in solid documentation and advocated collecting data firsthand in the field. He knew also that cultural evolution did not stop with modern society. In his reconstruction of evolutionary stages, Morgan placed modern monogamous marriage at the fifth, and final stage of development, but he did not believe that progress would end at this point. He observed that additional changes would occur even to the point where there would be equality between the sexes ([1877] 1963:499). He saw this eventuality not necessarily as a matter of direct change in the family itself while other institutions stood still, but as an indirect result of changes in those other institutions.

The development schemes of Morgan, Tylor and others were all flawed in some way. Some cultures and institutions did not fit their assigned categories well. Some evolutionists did not allow for the borrowing of ideas and technology between cultures, which would have disturbed the idea that cultures develop in a vacuum. Perhaps the most serious problem was in the quality of their data collected by untrained observers. Both Morgan and Tylor realized this fact and tried to compensate for it. Culture comparison must be based on accurate information gained by fieldwork, or the entire enterprise fails. Nevertheless, they both did quality work and advanced the comparative view.

The evolutionist approach died by 1900, but was reborn in the 1950s under the label of *neoevolutionism* and the leadership of Leslie White (1959). Neoevolutionism followed some of Morgan's ideas regarding the relationship between technological development and energy capture (as exemplified by agriculture, which increased food supply, or, today, by converting oil to gasoline) and culture development. It was based on much better field data after a half-century of professional fieldwork and was a much more sophisticated and productive enterprise than its predecessor.

SURVIVAL TASKS AND SOCIOCULTURAL COMPLEXITY

Alan Barnard (2000:57) identifies three common types of cultural comparison: illustrative, global, and controlled. *Illustrative comparison* draws on ethnographic data to illustrate a point about similarities and differences as we did in our discussion of poverty in three different settings in chapter 3. *Global comparison* uses statistical techniques to discover correlations among data in a sample of cultures drawn from a large database such as the Human Relations Area Files.[1] *Controlled comparison* is used to compare a limited number of cultures on a limited set of variables. All three of these types of comparison will be utilized in this section as we construct a general model of increasing sociocultural complexity in which basic *survival tasks become increasingly elaborated, and society becomes more complex in structure and content.* This is in fact a neoevolutionary classification that uses a culture's subsistence base as the principal criterion for classification. What we are attempting to accomplish by this approach is to reduce the great variety of cultures in the world to intellectually manageable proportions. By doing so, we further develop our framework of understanding.

All cultures must solve certain inherently human problems. All cultures must produce, distribute, and consume food; control sexual access to women; establish means of social control; and deal with the supernatural. These are universal problems on which we can base cross-cultural comparison. There are other universals as well, but they fall outside the scope of the present discussion. With this approach, we can trace the growth of culture globally through stages of development in which solving these universal problems becomes a more complex undertaking.

Adaptive Strategies

We live in such a complex, technologically driven society that it is hard to imagine that for most of our existence on the earth we have struggled to survive in an environment over which we have no control. We did not begin our earthly sojourn millennia ago as noble hunters courageously facing deadly predators, or as brilliant inventors of technology, but as lowly scavengers of lion-kills and as foragers for fruits and other seasonally available food. Gradually, however, we began to develop our technology, by excelling at making stone projectile points, and much later by domesticating plants and animals, a breakthrough that allowed us to produce food at an ever-increasing rate. Because of our ability to learn, we are able to live in an incredibly wide variety of environments with widely varying capacities to support human life. While our basic needs are the same everywhere, each environment presents a different challenge to our adaptive ability.

For thousands of years all humans lived a nomadic life, following herds of game and the seasonal ripening of foods. Today there are a few remaining nomadic groups, or bands, in places like southern Africa (for example, the San were discussed in chapter 4), the Arctic, and Australia. *Bands* are comprised essentially of small groups of independently operating families who forage for seasonal plants and hunt game for protein. Thus, they depend traditionally on hunting and gathering techniques of food production. The bands that exist today are not direct descendants of the original nomads and they live in marginal environments in contrast to the originals who lived in much richer locations. Today's bands live on land that has a low *carrying capacity,* that is, the land supports a very low *biomass* (the totality of life forms that can exist on it). Thus, the carrying capacity sets limits to their adaptation. It does not follow that this limitation determines the content of their culture, only that a low carrying capacity predicts a small population and less sociocultural complexity. The snow fields of the Arctic and the searing sands of the African desert may be similar in their low carrying capacity and result in broadly similar human adaptive strategies, but the customs and beliefs of the inhabitants of these two regions are quite different.

Because of their small size, bands do not require a highly structured society but rely instead on face-to-face relationships based on a common set of customs and beliefs. Although loosely organized, these families are highly dependent on each other for survival. When any one member of a family kills an animal, it is shared among all members of the family and with all other families in the group according to *rules of distribution*. These rules are customary understandings about who gets what piece of meat, and the method of distribution usually depends on how closely related the recipient is to the hunter who makes the kill. The products of foraging are, in most cases, more often a family matter without obligation to share with other families.

Our adaptive focus changed dramatically some ten thousand years ago with the domestication of plants and animals. We gained control over grains and roots, cows, pigs, sheep, and goats. In doing so we converted the carrying capacity of the land into more usable energy in the form of food production. The dramatic consequences of this development are referred to as the Neolithic Revolution because it changed human life forever. Horticulture (gardening, as opposed to large-scale agriculture) requires people to stay at home and to invest energy and resources in working the land. This sedentary village life leads to higher population concentrations that require a more complex sociocultural organization to order a more complex social life effectively. While still based on *kinship* (a relationship formed on the basis of blood or marriage ties), other associations known as *sodalities* cut across kinship systems to counteract kinship loyalties that could potentially split villages. They foster social solidarity as well as exact punishments on those who seriously violate norms and morals.

A *clan* is a sodality that loosely organizes a kinship group whose members *believe* that they are descendants of a common, mythical ancestor, but they cannot directly trace their relationship to the clan founder; they just claim it by telling a myth about how their clan was created. A *lineage,* by contrast, is a kinship group whose members can demonstrate their relationship to an actual, common ancestor. *Age grades* organize males and females who are within a narrow age range of each other into a cohesive group whose members progress through a series of age grades together. Each age grade has certain privileges and responsibilities, and members of an age grade are required to work together regardless of their lineage membership.

A *chiefdom* is an organized group whose level of development falls between that of a tribe and a state. Like tribes, they are based on kinship, but they are more formally organized; like states, whose organizing system is hierarchical, and a centralized body of members has authority, chiefdoms have *offices,* especially the office of chief. This is an enduring status, often inherited, which centralizes power and authority beyond that seen at the tribal level. The principal mechanism behind the chief's power is a system of *redistribution* in which commoners provide surplus produce to the chief who then can redistribute it as needed. This places him in control of important resources that he can use to bolster his power. His legitimacy is backed by religious sanction. The chief presides over a multivillage political and economic body; this body operates at yet a higher level of social complexity.

Agricultural innovations such as irrigation and terracing systems marked another surge in food production resulting in still larger populations. The food supply was sufficient to support full-time specialists such as priests, warriors, and bureaucrats who did not produce their own food. As a result of increased food production, as well as territorial expansion, still another level of social complexity was reached, the *state.* The Inca (Peru), Maya (Central America), Aztec (Mexico), and ancient Egypt were early states. With the state, power and authority were further centralized. Laws were made and enforced by the state. Differences in social status developed into social classes, and kinship became increasingly less important. These general developments in expanded food production, population increase, and more complex urban social life are reflected in the ways in which universal human needs are met.

Controlling Sexuality and Sexual Reproduction

Human sexuality is potentially disruptive to group life because conflict or violence can erupt over issues associated with sexual relationships, including jealousy, proprietary rights, and paternity. Every society attempts to control sexual expression and sexual reproduction in some way (Middleton 2002). Incest taboos, for example, are universal. The strongest incest prohibitions apply to members of the nuclear family, siblings and parents, but usually extend outward from this unit to include varying degrees of kinship. Some cultures allow first cousins to marry, while others do not. We commonly assign primary control of sexuality and sexual reproduction to the institutions of marriage and family. In spite of universal controls over sexual reproduction through marriage and incest taboos, a universally accurate definition of marriage remains elusive. In general, marriage includes *economic cooperation, social legitimacy* of offspring, and *sexual access.* But these three characteristics do not always occur together and should be considered as independent of each other unless otherwise demonstrated. Yet expanding a definition to fit every type of union observed around the world risks reducing the definition to a useless generality. Burton Pasternak and Carol and Melvin Ember suggest that we give up trying to discover an ultimate definition and deal with "*stable mated* relationships that are in fact universal in humans. That is, at any given time most adults in the world are in a reasonably stable relationship with another adult, and should the relationship be terminated, seek and enter a new relationship" (1997:107). Also, looking beyond definitions, Ward Goodenough (1970:12–13) suggests that we look at the problem humans are trying to solve, which in the case of marriage is "the right of sexual access to women." This is the approach we take in this section.

Regardless of the existence of some quite rare forms of marriage, the overall picture of marriage types is quite clear. Global comparison indicates that 82 percent of societies are *polygynous* (allow more than one wife), 18 percent are *monogamous* (allow only one spouse), and .05 percent are *polyandrous* (more than one husband) (Murdock 1949:28). Labeling a society polygynous does not mean that all marriages in that group are polygynous, only that such marriages are permitted, and perhaps encouraged. In fact, only about a third of the marriages, on the average, are actually polygynous because most men cannot afford them. Such marriages often suggest significant variations in wealth and prestige in such a culture.

Controlling sexual access is not just a problem of curbing desire, or protecting a female from unwanted advances, but more often one of protecting an economic asset and family honor. Marriage is seen in many places as a political and economic transaction between groups and not one based on individual love and physical attraction. When Goodenough says that marriage is about the right of sexual access, he has in mind such transactions. In these systems, female virginity is often equated with economic value and family honor. If virginity can be guaranteed, then rights in children will be clear and indisputable.

Some cultures go to the extreme to ensure female purity, and it should be noted that the procedures discussed here are not necessarily forced on girls or women. Restriction of sexual access to a woman by anyone other than her husband (to preserve virginity and to guarantee the legitimacy of heirs) is attained by female genital mutilation, FGM, which includes a number of practices of surgically altering female genitals. Two examples of FGM are clitoridectomy, when young girls have their clitoris or hood of their clitoris removed (which eliminates feelings of pleasure during sexual relations), and infibulation—removing the labia majora of the vagina—and sewing the vulva shut, leaving open a small hole in order to eliminate urine and menses. In addition to a high value being placed on the virginity of the bride, at the time of marriage there is a *wealth transfer,* or *bride price,* exchanged for the woman, which establishes rights and duties between husband and wife *and* between the two families and their kin.

Given such emphasis on reproduction and the rights to children, it should not be surprising that the most common reason for divorce globally is that the wife has borne no children in whom the husband would have rights; that is, it is (assumed) *female* infertility if no heirs are produced (Frayzer 1985:105). Another common reason for divorce globally is when a woman has extramarital sex, which also muddies the issue of legitimacy, if any children are conceived.

Some cultures are fairly permissive of sexual behavior. The Canela of the Amazon Basin (South America) (Crocker and Crocker 1994), for example, traditionally use premarital and extramarital sex to foster solidarity and to prevent potential conflict over sexual access. Instead of severely restricting sexual contact, they reduce sexual tension by widely sharing sexual partners among married and unmarried members of the group; married women have sex with men, other than their husbands, as well as with their husbands. Also, the Canela practice sequential sex: in certain ceremonies women have sex sequentially with different men. Jealousy is a rarely expressed feeling. Note that the Canela are not concerned about ownership or economic rights in children and are unconcerned about illegitimacy. Honor is not linked with virginity. The Canela have neither property nor wealth to protect in marriage.

As indicated by the previous examples, cultures vary in their attitudes toward premarital and extramarital sex. Restrictions are most likely to apply to extramarital sex and to women; men are given much more freedom in both premarital and extramarital sex. Gwen Broude and Sara Greene (1976) found that of a sample of 141 cultures, about one-third permit premarital sex, about one-third require females to be virgins at marriage, and about one-third permit premarital sex if it is practiced discreetly. These data reflect normative attitudes and are not the result of direct observation of sexual behavior.

Band-level societies, having no concept of ownership and holding no land, do not feature tight controls on premarital sexual activity and virginity as economic assets. As property becomes more important at the tribal level, these issues may arise. There is, however, a great deal of cultural variation in this respect at the tribal level.

In cultures like that of the United States, the notion of romantic love as a motivation for marriage disconnects it from the need to make economic and political deals. The lack of emphasis on politically or economically connecting two families through marriage is related to industrialization and the rise of wage earners who own little property; children may be seen as economic liabilities rather than assets. The invention of better and more inexpensive birth control methods and the changing status of women also contribute to changing attitudes and practices. In some cultures, women's reproduction has come under government control to achieve the interest of the state. China, for example, has a one-child rule, whereby married couples are limited to having only one offspring.

Social Control

Our survival depends on a minimally effective degree of group cooperation. As noted in chapter 3, we endeavor to meet this goal by coordinating—controlling—the activity and values of the individual with those of the group and to punish individuals who fail to conform. All cultures, in other words, must exert a measure of social control. Socialization is the primary and normally most effective mechanism of social control because it produces adults who accept and internalize the values and understandings of the group. Adults are self-monitoring individuals who voluntarily conform to *social norms*. Learning social roles, based for example on age and sex, early in life is an important part of the socialization process, because a social role defines both the rights and duties of individuals. Acting in voluntary compliance with cultural ideals and norms does not require corrective measures from authorities or friends and relatives. However, the socialization process is imperfect, and social life is complex enough that conflicts inevitably arise. Add social change to this mix and the group might experience difficulty even in deciding what comprises proper child rearing and role definition.

Conflict and deviation from what is accepted by the group as normal are inherent in human social life, and societies therefore must devise mechanisms of social control to deal with these phenomena. *Indirect control* refers to control measures, such as gossip and ridicule, which are intended to undermine a person's public standing and pressure her to conform. Many cultures feature *corporate* lineages, meaning that the lineage acts as a cohesive unit and that it assumes responsibility for the behavior of its members; the entire lineage is thus held accountable for a single member's or family's transgressions. Religious beliefs are indirect but powerful sources of social conformity as they define moral behavior and threaten punishment by a supernatural being. Where there is ancestor worship, individuals fear that their moral transgressions may bring upon them the vengeful wrath of ancestors who are the guardians of morality.

Indirect mechanisms of social control work sufficiently well in smaller societies based on face-to-face relationships but are unable, alone, to handle the more complex issues that accompany increasing sociocultural complexity. Power and authority become more centralized in chiefdoms; in states there are lawmakers and bureaucracies that set laws and regulations and there are courts, police, and military forces that support them. These *formal* means of social control do not displace informal means, but simply overlay them.

Beliefs in the Supernatural

Our ceaseless quest for the meaning of those conditions of life that puzzle us and that are beyond our control compels us to search for answers via beliefs about the supernatural. So elemental to human life is the supernatural that Edward Tylor defined religion simply as a belief in the supernatural no matter how institutionalized and ritually elaborated it may become. Our need for explanation and meaning is both cognitive and emotional. The cognitive function establishes causes and meanings and explains the origin of people and the nature of the world. The emotional function allays anxiety, focuses emotions, and fosters group identity and solidarity. These functions are served by myths (stories that reveal the truth about the origins of worldly things, such as animals) and rituals (the acting out of a myth for some purpose, e.g., to recognize the passage of seasons) that work at both individual and group levels.

Robert Tonkinson (1978:14) comments on the role that dreamtime beliefs (beliefs about the ongoing creation of the world) play in the everyday lives of Mardudjara Aborigines of Australia.

> Their cosmology not only accounts for the origins and form of their world, but also binds them closely to one another, to the land, all living things, and to the realm of the spiritual beings who control the power on which life itself is held dependent. The sum of these bonds is to the Aborigines a logically unified order, in which all will be well if only they live according to the rules laid down by the spiritual beings who created their universe.

Dreamtime is both a spiritual belief and a prescription for everyday social life. It gives the Aborigines their worldview. It is a rich and complex set of beliefs that guides and gives meaning to the lives of these technologically simple nomadic bands of the western desert.

The evolution of religious organization follows generally the same trajectory from simple to complex we have traced thus far with the other survival tasks. Specifically, the development is from part-time specialist to full-time specialist. A *shaman* is a part-time specialist who is a curer and diviner. He is the one who is called on in sickness and death, or community misfortune, to divine the cause and to prescribe medicines or rituals to remedy the problem. He may have prestige, but he still has to support himself and his family in much the same way as other members of the community. Priests are full-time specialists who organize and conduct rituals, interpret the meaning of events, and advise rulers. Priesthoods support the state and can be quite powerful and influential in state matters. A state religion helps to maintain unity among the many social elements of a complex society and supports state expansion. The development of more complex organizations, however, does not displace other forms of religion or religious practitioners, but overlays them. We must caution again that while these categories are useful in effectively organizing our thoughts about the diverse kinds of religions and religious organizations, they are also imperfect matches with reality and must be used with caution.

Wealth, Power, and Prestige

One way to measure increasing sociocultural complexity is the degree to which a culture becomes internally differentiated with respect to individual access to wealth, power, and prestige (Weber 1946 [1922]). *Wealth* refers to the accumulation of economic resources, *power* to the ability to impose one's will on another, and *prestige* to the amount of social esteem one receives. Differences along these dimensions describe conditions of *social inequality* and *social stratification,* that is, the hierarchical arrangement of groups of people. To chart the evolution of sociocultural complexity along this dimension is to describe the rise of social inequality in human populations. These three variables should be considered analytically separate from each other, because they do not necessarily occur together. A village headman may have a great deal of prestige, a little power, and virtually no wealth. "Big men" in the Pacific are those who amass wealth for the purposes of political wheeling and dealing, ultimately giving away most of their wealth for the social esteem it brings them.

With the development of sociocultural complexity, society becomes increasingly segmented into a greater number of roles and statuses; there is an increase in social units, specialization, and functional integration. In other words, increased complexity means there are more specialized parts of society that must work together to make the system effective. While there are more positions of wealth, power, and prestige available to be filled at each level of complexity, they are still limited relative to the greater number of people to occupy them. At the band level there is virtually no social differentiation along these dimensions because there are none available. This is why bands are regarded as *egalitarian* on this measure of complexity. Through the tribal, or *rank,* level, we are speaking of differentiation at the individual level. Individuals may have great prestige, but there is still little differentiation in wealth and power. Chiefdoms and early states are *stratified* societies containing social classes such as nobles and commoners. Nobility often possess all three characteristics of social differentiation. Stratified societies have groups of people, or certain categories of them, that are hierarchically arranged with respect to wealth, power, and prestige. In modern nations, such as the United States, social classes are defined mainly by economic resources and are hierarchically arranged into lower, middle, and upper.

This overview of the evolution of sociocultural complexity anchored in the universal jobs that we must accomplish to survive facilitates our conceptual control of cultural similarities and differences. This developmental scheme rests essentially on the use of comparison on a global scale. *Cultures at one level are more similar in certain key respects than those at different levels, but there is variety within each level related to specific local ecological and historical circumstances.* This approach does not rule out the impact of extensive cultural borrowing among cultures that in fact has taken place from the beginning.

CONTROLLED COMPARISON: McWORLD

While Barnard (2000) identified three basic types of comparison, Thomas Gregor and Donald Tuzin (2001:15) suggest that there really is an "unbounded set of comparison strategies." They note further that, "*all* anthropology is comparative" (p. 2). The extent to which we can establish *laws* of culture and society through comparison is open for debate, but by informed comparison we certainly can deepen our understanding of the universal and local expressions of humanity. As an example, Gregor and Tuzin (2001) note that for nearly a century anthropologists have recognized striking similarities between the cultures of Melanesia and Amazonia, two areas widely separated by history and geography. In this controlled comparison the researchers do not try to establish the ancient origins of these similarities, nor do they assume that the two culture areas are similar because they share the same evolutionary stage. Instead, they use comparisons to sort how they are different yet similar, in order to learn more about both. For example, the two areas display similarities in ideas and rituals relating to gender, sex, and the body. At the center of this cultural complex is the men's cult, with secret rituals of initiation and procreation that exclude women. Those who violate the cult are punished by gang rape or death. The myths that explain the origin and reason for the cult are also similar in spite of the great geographical distance between them. Is this similarity due to ancient contact between them, or to similar "solutions" to similar problems? Although the answer is unknown, the latter case is the more likely.

In these types of studies, scholars investigate various aspects of the central theme, but all do not use the same comparative technique or draw identical conclusions. What does emerge in the absence of a common conclusion, however, is an enhancement of their understanding of both regions and of variations within each region. Among the methodological cautions that emerge in this type of comparison are the:

1. necessity of defining the historical, political, and economic *context* of the cultures compared;

2. necessity of including *both* the *similarities and differences* among cultures;

3. importance of understanding how customs and institutions *relate* to other elements within each culture;

4. importance of not *essentializing* cultures as an inherently fixed entity;

5. importance of being aware of *surface similarities,* but *functional differences.*

This list can be considered a basic roster of checkpoints to consider when making a comparison, and as such it has wide application in comparative studies. To illustrate them, we return to the story of the global expansion of McDonald's.

We saw in the first chapter that being confronted with unfamiliar food in an unfamiliar setting can contribute to culture shock. We become quite attached to certain foods in our routine diet, and individually we exhibit varying degrees of tolerance for exotic cuisine. Food is consumed in a social context and, like drinking beer in Botswana or virtually anywhere else, is usually viewed as a social event. Each culture generates a normative set of food categories that arranges and values food for daily consumption, for special social occasions, and even for ritual purposes. A famous and widespread classification is one that divides foods into "hot" and "cold" categories (not necessarily dependent on temperature or spiciness but on folk classifications of the cause and treatment of illness). A person must balance her ingestion of food between the two categories under various circumstances, usually to prevent or to cure an illness. Given, then, our human tendency to be committed to certain foods as a matter of local availability, social meanings, and taste familiarity, how can a U.S. fast-food restaurant with limited menu succeed internationally?

McDonald's international operation offers an instructive case for cultural comparison, because it is based on a uniform system of production and delivery standardized in the United States, but subsequently exported across international cultural boundaries (Watson 1997). Service is quick and reliable; facilities are clean; the food is fresh; and prices are reasonable. Although the menu originally consisted mainly of burgers, fries, and beverages, McDonald's has expanded menu choices to include salads, chicken selections, breakfast items, and desserts. The menu changes little cross-culturally except for some provision for local customs and beliefs. For example, in India, the menu includes vegetarian items, and even the mayonnaise does not contain any eggs (http://mcdonaldsindia.net/about/faq.htm). McDonald's restaurants in other countries show other slight modifications, but otherwise the menu is the same (fries are universally accepted) and even new items must be standardized.[2] One unanticipated success is the cross-cultural acceptance of the cleanliness of the toilets and kitchen, which appears to have sparked a hygiene movement in competitive restaurants. Customers in many countries also find the service with a smile approach a welcome change from the routine, but in other places the smile in such cases is suspect. Although McDonald's prices are often too high for frequent visits by members of the working class, they are lower than some competitors' prices (in some countries there is a shortage of middle-range restaurants).

What other factors account for McDonald's successful expansion? Timing is one important part of it (Watson 1997:14–22). The restaurants are being introduced in countries where an affluent middle class and a youth culture are emerging to demand consumer goods and as national governments loosen controls on foreign businesses—in other words McDonald's has entered the scene at the right historical moment. The rise of a youth culture and an affluent middle class in many countries usually signals changing family values. Such changes do not mean necessarily just visiting McDonald's, but opening up as well to transnationalism (Watson 1997:1–14). These countries are striving to become modern and progressive, and McDonald's symbolizes change. As Sidney Mintz points out, "The introduction of privately owned and managed retail facilities for the sale and consumption of new, and different foods, on the premises, or off, can reflect fundamental change in the social circumstances of the conduct of daily life" (1997:193). In order to better grasp these changes, Mintz notes it is necessary to develop in detail more knowledge of the intrafamilial decision making regarding visits to fast-food outlets in these countries (p. 196). Furthermore, it is important to understand the dynamic economic landscape in each country. For example, in China, more condominiums are being built and more people are driving cars. These changes have inspired McDonald's to open drive-thru outlets in China (Griffith 2008) and to boost its investment in China by about 25 percent in 2010 (Chicago Business 2010).

While the subtitle of James Watson's book, *Golden Arches East: McDonald's in East Asia*, implies a homogeneous region, the articles contained in it reveal that East Asian cultures are not all alike—an assumption that they are is a fallacy of essentializing—and they do not all respond to McDonald's the same way, because how McDonald's is received depends partly on how it is related to other aspects of culture. While each McDonald's restaurant operates according to the same standardized system in all countries, it serves somewhat different functions in different countries. All McDonald's restaurants are half-owned by local managers. Managers work hard to make themselves an integral part of the community by participating in various events and visiting schools. In China, Aunt and Uncle McDonald work as receptionists at the restaurant, but also record children's names and birthdays, send them cards on their birthdays, and visit them at school (Yan 1997:60–61). These efforts are calculated to win long-term customer loyalty. This community orientation is duplicated to a degree in Seoul, Korea, but here there is a substantial measure of ambivalence and resistance to McDonald's as an intrusive, non-national, force—a symbol of cultural imperialism.

In China, going to McDonald's is a significant social event. Not only does it reflect one's affluence and progressive values, but also McDonald's is appropriated for family rituals and special occasions. Breakfast is the most popular meal at McDonald's in Hong Kong where it is almost a routine part of the daily round for office workers in a culture long dominated by international business interests. In other places the restaurant may be a gathering spot for women, or it may be a part of a leisure system where affluent young people hang out for longer periods of time after eating than do most customers. The same institution thus has both different and similar functions in different countries. Eric Schlosser (2002:225–252) also writes about McDonald's international operation (however, the book is mostly about the U.S.), as well as that of other fast-food franchises, and provides information about its successful operation in Germany, a modern, industrialized country. As noted earlier, McDonald's symbolism is not solely about the United States, but about the wider phenomenon of transnationalism and globalization and how it impinges on various local cultures.

COMPARISON IN APPLIED ANTHROPOLOGY

Anthropologists seek to combine the specific and the general in a unified view of human life. In spite of their focus on specific programs of change, applied anthropologists must do the same, and more. In addition to their undergraduate training in anthropology, and thus their exposure to the combined perspective, they also acquire knowledge of methods and principles in applied anthropology. The analytical landmarks listed in the following chapter derive from the comparison of numerous case studies of culture change, and are certainly important dynamics that the applied anthropologist should understand. The comparative method is useful also in building a body of information on principles or best practices in the practical realm. As early as 1952, Spicer wrote about the kinds of unintended consequences found in applied programs, and Goodenough (1963) wrote about the types of problems and opportunities encountered in practice. Other compilations of practices based on the cross-cultural comparison of many cases have appeared (Ervin 2005: 233–242, Higgins and Paredes 2000, van Willigen 2002). Thus, practicing anthropologists can now draw on an ample cross-cultural fund of practical experience as they cycle between the general and the specific.

General principles always need to be adapted to local conditions, and it is imperative to discover the problems and solutions from the local viewpoint. Doing so is more likely to result in a successful program.

CONCLUSION

The early attempts to classify newly discovered peoples as degenerate were inadequate and represent ethnocentric efforts to extend to new discoveries old ideas about the nature of the world (especially ideas about morality) and the people in it. As the idea of science began to mature during the Renaissance and the Enlightenment eras, scholars began to think more of progress than degeneration. Early attempts by classical evolutionists to arrange cultures hierarchically by levels of progress failed largely because of poor data and a lack of understanding of how cultures work. Tylor and Morgan, however, were more perceptive than most early evolutionists and both made lasting theoretical and methodological contributions to the comparative perspective. Cultural comparison is a necessary and vital approach that must balance the uniqueness of a culture with the universal features of cultures. These universals furnish us with a common and convenient place from which to launch cultural comparison.

Cultural comparison can be combined with an evolutionary, or developmental, approach that presents us with a general view of how culture has developed globally toward greater sociocultural complexity and helps us to organize the diverse cultures into useful categories that stimulate further inquiry. Neoevolutionists were able, after a half-century of solid fieldwork, to devise a new developmental scheme based on a global comparison of subsistence strategies that was more successful than the early efforts. Taking certain universal survival tasks as a basis of comparison, we have seen how such tasks have become increasingly elaborated and complex as we move into modern statehood and finally to the global village as suggested in the controlled comparison of McDonald's in East Asia. The McDonald's example shows the value of the critical points raised by Gregor and Tuzin in making effective comparisons and heading off some sources of methodological error. The comparative point of view in applied anthropology has established a solid cross-cultural base for the development of accepted practice.

Critical Thinking

1. What is wrong with the common idea that humans are evolving toward some higher level of existence?

2. Relate the concepts of adaptive focus, adaptive strategy, and level of sociocultural integration with each other. Give examples.

3. To what degree do you think globalization is possible or desirable? Are there limits? Back up your thoughts with several examples.

Notes

[1] The Human Relations Area Files, Inc., is an internationally recognized organization in the field of cultural anthropology. It is a nonprofit consortium of universities, colleges, and research agencies in more than 30 countries. The HRAF Collection of Ethnography currently contains nearly 1,000,000 pages of information on cultures of the world.

[2] Hindus, however, have protested fries being cooked in animal fat.

Chapter Six

Meeting the Challenge of Global Issues

All over the world, throughout the 1990s, protesters damaged McDonald's restaurants (Schlosser 2001:243–244). The protestors represented a wide variety of interests—farmers, environmentalists, labor unionists, health advocates, animal rights supporters, and nationalists against foreign intrusion. Why has McDonald's become the target of these demonstrations? What is going on here? The most commonly offered answer to this question is that the fast-food industry, being uniquely a product of the United States and symbolic of U.S. international economic success, is a convenient target for those who resent or are threatened by U.S. success. There is no doubt some truth to this simple argument, but on closer examination what does it really explain? Another answer suggests that these reactions are more about *cultural imperialism,* the domination of Western, particularly North American culture than about economic success. Thus, the flood of CDs, jeans, and fast food that washes over the world is rejected because it threatens local cultural identity. Again, there is some truth to this assertion, but neither answer is sufficiently detailed to match the complex reality of the *global village,* a concept that suggests that the diverse cultures of the world are linked and reliant on each other.

Globalization is a vague and sweeping term that nevertheless refers to real processes at work on a global level. These processes have intensified following the end of the cold war in the late 1980s. Generally, globalization refers to the increasingly dense web of economic and political ties and increasing cultural exchange among nations; it suggests that a world culture—a *homogenization* of cultures—is emerging as a consequence, that the process of homogenization is inevitable and irreversible, that we have perhaps reached another level of sociocultural complexity, and that cultural diversity will disappear. While we cannot here delve into the many dimensions of the globalization process, we can suggest how our framework of understanding can help us to develop a more comprehensive view of this multifaceted phenomenon that McDonald's symbolizes for so many people around the world.

Watson's book on McDonald's in East Asia is a compilation of different studies made by researchers who had firsthand, extended experience in that region. Taken as a whole, these studies constitute a controlled comparison of McDonald's in different places. Thus, it uses the anthropological strategy of extended, firsthand contact and a comparative perspective to understand both the local experience and a wider variety of experiences with McDonald's in different cultures. Although the quality and amount of detailed ethnographic work varies among the studies, all raise important issues that can lead to additional, better-targeted research.

As a result of these studies we see that those who embrace Westernization—at least to a degree—are the developing affluent classes and emerging youth cultures in a number of different East Asian countries. At the same time we see ambivalence and fear, for example, many Koreans fear that McDonald's represents a foreign corruption of Korean culture. However, we cannot essentialize cultures—an "Eastern" culture, or even a national culture—because there are class and regional differences within them. This means that we need to identify who is visiting McDonald's and who is protesting and why.

Much of the cultural dynamics Watson's anthology illustrates is well known by anthropologists because of their own and others' long experience with culture contact (as noted especially in chapter 4). Here are some analytical landmarks that help us understand what happens in the process of culture change:

1. Change does *not* usually *proceed* steadily *in one direction;* it encounters resistance and unexpected consequences.

2. Change is an *interactive process* between two or more cultures, no matter which appears dominant or subordinate.

3. Western ideals of *progress and development* are *not universally accepted* as a good.

4. Change is *experienced differentially* by different segments of the local population.

5. Cultures selectively *accept, reject, or modify* elements of other cultures.

6. Change interacts with the local cognitive and emotional styles; it has *symbolic value.*

Examples of all of these principles can be found operating in the cultures studied in Watson's compilation. We need to remember as we address these issues that when we speak of cultures we are *reifying* culture, that is, making a concept a living actor; whereas, in reality, a culture is learned behavior enacted on a daily basis by individuals and groups who are not all occupying the same status, role, or social class, nor are they sharing the same religion or same sect of a religion. Individuals and groups act, cultures do not. Not all individuals and groups respond in the same way to change, and this is where solid fieldwork is required.

These analytical landmarks bear directly on applied projects of change. If we do not acquire a detailed understanding of a group, how can we hope to develop more enlightened and successful programs of change? Projects that fail in this regard are doomed from the start. This perspective has been difficult for Westerners to grasp because they have felt that "progress" has a magical quality that everyone, cross-culturally, will automatically embrace. This, as we have seen, is not the case. Fortunately, this attitude has begun to change, and the anthropological contribution is becoming better appreciated.

From the Western viewpoint, there is the implicit notion that global culture will be a Western culture based on liberal economics and political democracy. All of this remains to be seen, but one thing that will not happen in this century is the disappearance of cultural diversity. Who would want diversity to vanish anyway? In spite of the difficulties sometimes attendant to understanding another culture, cultural diversity offers a reservoir of cultural possibility and cultural heritage that can enrich our lives even as it sometimes confuses us. Cultural diversity will not disappear because culture is dynamic and adaptive to ever-changing conditions that are not the same for every culture. At the same time, cultures will continue to borrow from each other and they will create new *syncretisms,* that is, new cultural combinations in cuisine, the arts, religion, and worldviews that can revitalize all cultures.

Yet, these are also fertile times for the politics of hatred and divisiveness. The culture wars mentioned in the introduction are very much with us on national and global levels. Assertions and counter assertions about heritage and ethnic purity, about East versus West, and we and they mark the day (Foster 1991). These contests—the politics of identity—involve varying degrees of ignorance or understanding of others, but they are mostly about differential power and wealth expressed symbolically—the idiom of cultural difference. Culture and ethnicity in this context become the bases for political protests and actions; they are the rationale, not the cause.

Terrorism is the shadowy and bloody side of hatred and divisiveness. It is an extreme idiom of poverty, and political and economic alienation. It does no good to label terrorists as evil and to try to eliminate them unless you also attack the root causes that spawned them in the first place. And this act would demand a higher level of cultural understanding and sensitivity than we customarily find in popular discussions of terrorism. The U.S. has consistently erred in this regard, too often relying on technology rather than on a well-grounded knowledge of other cultures.

Many observers today have expressed a deep concern over the power of the Internet to cater increasingly to narrow interests and over the effect that the proliferating number of TV channels might have on reinforcing a narrow view of the world. Will these technological advancements dampen our willingness to engage with others? Will they reinforce microscopic differences at the cost of our commonality?

We are no less challenged by human diversity than we were a century ago. We do not lack the tools by which to meet this challenge, but whether or not we have the political will is another question.

Bibliography

Agar, Michael. 1973. *Ripping and Running: A Formal Ethnography of Urban Heroin Addicts.* New York: Seminar Press.

———. 1980. *The Professional Stranger: An Informal Introduction to Ethnography.* New York: Academic Press.

Altorki, Soraya, and Camilia Fawzi El-Solh. 1984. *Arab Women in the Field: Studying Your Own Society.* Syracuse, NY: Syracuse University Press.

Alverson, Marianne. 1987. *Under African Sun.* Chicago: University of Chicago Press.

Anderson, Barbara Gallatin. 1990. *First Fieldwork: The Misadventures of an Anthropologist.* Long Grove, IL: Waveland Press.

Barnard, Alan. 2000. *History and Theory in Anthropology.* Cambridge: Cambridge University Press.

Barth, Fredrik. [1969] 1998. *Ethnic Groups and Boundaries: The Social Organization of Culture Difference.* Long Grove, IL: Waveland Press.

Belmonte, Thomas. 1989. *The Broken Fountain,* 2d ed. New York: Columbia University Press.

Berry, John. 1976. *Human Ecology and Cognitive Style.* New York: Halsted.

Bodley, John. 1990. *Victims of Progress,* 3d ed. Mountain View, CA: Mayfield.

Bohannan, Laura (see Bowen, Elenore Smith).

Bourdieu, Pierre. 1984. *Distinction: A Social Critique of the Judgment of Taste,* Richard Nice (trans.). Cambridge: Cambridge University Press.

Bowen, Elenore Smith (Laura Bohannan). [1954] 1964. *Return to Laughter.* New York: Harper & Row.

Briggs, Jean. 1970. *Never in Anger: Portrait of an Eskimo Family.* Cambridge: Harvard University Press.

Broude, Gwen J., and Sara J. Greene. 1976. "Cross-Cultural Codes on Twenty Sexual Attitudes and Practices." *Ethnology* 15: 409–30.

Brown, Donald. 1991. *Human Universals.* New York: McGraw Hill.

Burkey, Richard M. 1978. *Ethnic and Racial Groups: The Dynamics of Dominance.* Menlo Park, CA: Cummings.

Butler, Thomas. 1992. "The Ends of History: Balkan Culture and Catastrophe." *Washington Post.* August 30, p. C3.

Campbell, Bernard G. 1987. *Humankind Emerging,* 5th ed. Glenview, IL: Scott, Foresman.

Carmichael, Stokely, and Charles Hamilton. 1967. *Black Power: The Politics of Liberation in America.* New York: Vintage.

111

Chagnon, Napoleon A. 1992. *Yanomamo*, 4th ed. New York: Harcourt, Brace, Jovanovich.

Chambers, Erve. 2010. *Native Tours: The Anthropology of Travel and Tourism*, 2d ed. Long Grove, IL: Waveland Press.

Chicago Business. 2010, January 29. "McDonald's to Boost Investment in China by 25% in 2010," http://www.chicagobusiness.com/cgi-bin/news.pl?id=36911 (retrieved March 15, 2010).

Clark, Kenneth. 1965. *Dark Ghetto: Dilemmas of Social Power*. New York: Harper.

Cole, Michael, John Gay, and D. W. Sharp. 1971. *The Cultural Context of Learning and Thinking*. New York: Basic Books.

Cole, Michael, and Barbara Means. 1981. *Comparative Studies of How People Think: An Introduction*. Cambridge: Harvard University Press.

Cornell, Stephen. 1988. *The Return of the Native*. New York: Oxford University Press.

Counts, David. [1990] 2000. "Too Many Bananas, Not Enough Pineapples, and No Watermelon at All: Three Object Lessons in Living with Reciprocity." In *Stumbling Toward Truth: Anthropologists at Work*, Philip R. DeVita (ed.), pp. 177–84. Long Grove, IL: Waveland Press.

Crocker, William, and Jean Crocker. 1994. *Canela: Bonding Through Kinship, Ritual, and Sex*. New York: Holt, Rinehart, and Winston.

Darby, John. 1976. *Conflict in Northern Ireland: The Development of a Polarised Community*. Dublin: Gill & Macmillan.

Darwin, Charles. [1859] 1997. *The Origin of Species*. New York: W.W. Norton & Co.

Deloria, Jr., Vine. 1969. *Custer Died for Your Sins*. New York: Macmillan.

DeVita, Philip R., ed. 1990. *The Humbled Anthropologist: Tales from the Pacific*. Belmont, CA: Wadsworth. Excerpts of this text reissued as *Stumbling Toward Truth: Anthropologists at Work*. Long Grove, IL: Waveland Press, 2000.

Draper, Patricia. 1975. "!Kung Women: Contrasts in Sexual Egalitarianism in Foraging and Sedentary Contexts." In *Toward an Anthropology of Women*, R. Reiter (ed.), pp. 77–109. New York: Monthly Review Press.

Dumont, Jean-Paul. [1978] 1992. *The Headman and I: Ambiguity and Ambivalence in the Fieldworking Experience*. Long Grove, IL: Waveland Press.

Ekman, Paul, ed. 1982. *Emotion in the Human Face*, 2d ed. Cambridge: Cambridge University Press.

Erchak, Gerald M. 1992. *The Anthropology of Self and Behavior*. New Brunswick, NJ: Rutgers University Press.

Ervin, Alexander M. 2005. *Applied Anthropology: Tools and Perspectives for Contemporary Practice*. New York: Allyn & Bacon.

Feld, Steven. 1990. *Sound and Sentiment: Birds, Weeping, Poetics, and Song in Kaluli Expression*, 2d ed. Philadelphia: University of Pennsylvania Press.

Fernea, Elizabeth Warnock. [1976] 1988. *A Street in Marrakech: A Personal View of Women in Morocco*. Long Grove, IL: Waveland Press.

Foster, Robert J. 1991. "Making National Cultures in the Global Ecumene." *Annual Review of Anthropology* 20:235–60.

Frayzer, Suzanne G. 1985. *Varieties of Sexual Experience: An Anthropological Perspective on Human Sexuality*. New Haven, CT: HRAF Press.

Freilich, Morris, ed. 1968. *Marginal Natives: Anthropologists at Work*. New York: Harper & Row.

Geertz, Clifford. 1973. *The Interpretation of Cultures*. New York: Basic Books.

Golde, Peggy, ed. 1970. *Women in the Field: Anthropological Experiences*. Chicago: Aldine.

Goodenough, Ward. 1963. *Cooperation in Change: An Anthropological Approach to Community Development*. New York: Russell Sage Foundation.

———. 1970. *Description and Comparison in Cultural Anthropology*. Chicago: Aldine.

Gordon, Robert. 1992. *The Myth of Africa: The Making of a Namibian Underclass*. Boulder, CO: Westview.

Gould, Stephen J. 1981. *The Mismeasure of Man*. New York: Norton.

Graburn, Nelson H. H., ed. 1976. *Ethnic and Tourist Arts: Cultural Expressions from the Fourth World.* Berkeley: University of California Press.

Gregor, Thomas, and Donald Tuzin. 2001. *Gender in Amazonia and Melanesia: An Exploration of the Comparative Method.* Berkeley: University of California Press.

Griffith, Wally. 2008, August 15. "McDonalds Has Big Appetite for China," http://www.msnbc.msn.com/id/26226387/ns/business-cnbc_tv// (retrieved March 15, 2010).

Gwynne, Margaret A. 2003. *Applied Anthropology: A Career-Oriented Approach.* New York: Allyn & Bacon.

Hahn, Elizabeth. 1990. "Raising a Few Eyebrows in Tonga." In *The Humbled Anthropologist,* Philip DeVita (ed.), pp. 69–76. Belmont, CA: Wadsworth.

Hall, Edward. 1990. *Understanding Cultural Differences.* Yarmouth, ME: Intercultural Press.

Hammond, Dorothy, and Alta Jablow. [1970] 1992. *The Africa That Never Was.* Long Grove, IL: Waveland Press.

———. 1977. *The Myth of Africa.* New York: Library of Social Science.

Hannerz, Ulf. 1969. *Soulside.* New York: Columbia University Press.

Hanson, F. Allan. 1975. *Meaning in Culture.* London: Routledge & Kegan Paul.

Harris, Grace Gredys. 1978. *Casting Out Anger: Religion Among the Taita of Kenya.* Long Grove, IL: Waveland Press.

Hemming, John. [1978] 1987. *Red Gold: The Conquest of the Brazilian Indians.* New York: Macmillan.

Herskovits, Melville J. 1973. *Cultural Relativism: Perspectives in Cultural Pluralism.* New York: Random House (Vintage).

Higgins, Patricia J., and Anthony J. Paredes. 2000. *Classics of Practicing Anthropology: 1978–98.* Oklahoma City: Society for Applied Anthropology.

Holmberg, Allan R. "The Research and Development Approach to the Study of Change." *Human Organization* 17: 12–16.

Hufford, Mary, ed. 1994. *Conserving Culture: A New Discourse on Heritage.* Urbana: University of Illinois Press.

Jackson, Michael. 1989. *Paths Toward a Clearing: Radical Empiricism and Ethnographic Inquiry.* Bloomington: Indiana University Press.

Jordan, Ann T. 2003. *Business Anthropology.* Long Grove, IL. Waveland Press.

Kluckhohn, Clyde. 1960. *Mirror for Man.* New York: Fawcett/McGraw Hill.

Konner, Melvin. 1982. *The Tangled Wing: Biological Constraints of the Human Spirit.* New York: Harper & Row.

Kottak, Conrad P. 2001. *Anthropology: The Exploration of Human Diversity,* 9th ed. New York: McGraw-Hill.

Leacock, Eleanor Burke. 1963. "Introduction to Part I." In *Ancient Society,* by Lewis Henry Morgan, pp. Ii–I20. New York: World Publishing.

———. 1971. *The Culture of Poverty: A Critique.* New York: Simon & Schuster.

Lee, Dorothy. [1959] 1987. *Freedom and Culture.* Long Grove, IL: Waveland Press.

Levy, Robert I. 1973. *Tahitian: Mind and Experience in the Society Islands.* Chicago: University of Chicago Press.

Lewis, Oscar. 1959. *Five Families: Mexican Case Studies in the Culture of Poverty.* New York: Basic Books.

———. 1961. *The Children of Sanchez: Autobiography of a Mexican Family.* New York: Random House.

———. 1966. *La Vida: A Puerto Rican Family in the Culture of Poverty—San Juan and New York.* New York: Random House.

Liebow, Elliot. 1967. *Tally's Corner: A Study of Streetcorner Men.* Boston: Beacon.

Locke, John. [1690] 1970. *Essay Concerning Human Understanding.* Roger Woolhouse (ed.). New York: Penguin Books.

Lutz, Catherine. 1988. *Unnatural Emotions: Everyday Sentiment on a Micronesian Atoll and the Challenge to Western Theory.* Chicago: University of Chicago Press.

Lutz, Catherine A., and Jane L. Collins. 1993. *Reading "National Geographic."* Chicago: University of Chicago Press.

Malifijt, Annemarie de Waal. 1974. *Images of Man: A History of Anthropological Thought.* New York: Knopf.

Margolis, Maxine. 2000. *True to Her Nature: Changing Advice to American Women.* Long Grove, IL: Waveland Press.

Martin, Kay, and Barbara Voorhies. 1975. *Female of the Species.* New York: Columbia University Press.

Mascia-Lees, Frances E. 2010. *Gender and Difference in a Globalizing World: Twenty-First Century Anthropology.* Long Grove, IL: Waveland Press.

Maybury-Lewis, David. [1965] 1988. *The Savage and the Innocent.* Boston: Beacon Press.

Middleton, DeWight R. 1981. "The Organization of Ethnicity in Tampa." *Ethnic Groups* 3:281–306.

———. 1989. "Emotional Style: The Cultural Ordering of Emotions." *Ethos* 17:187–201.

———. 2002. *Exotics and Erotics: Human Cultural and Sexual Diversity.* Long Grove, IL: Waveland Press.

Mintz, Sidney W. 1997. "Swallowing Modernity." In *Golden Arches East: McDonald's in East Asia,* James Watson (ed.), pp. 183–200. Stanford, CA: Stanford University Press.

Mitchell, William E. 1987. *The Bamboo Fire: Field Work with the New Guinea Wape,* 2d ed. Long Grove, IL: Waveland Press.

Moffatt, Michael. 1989. *Coming of Age in New Jersey.* New Brunswick: Rutgers University Press.

Molnar, Steve. 1983. *Human Variation: Races, Types, and Ethnic Groups,* 2d ed. Englewood Cliffs, NJ: Prentice-Hall.

Moore, Joan. 1976. *Mexican Americans.* Englewood Cliffs, NJ: Prentice-Hall.

Morgan, Lewis Henry. [1851] 1962. *League of the Iroquois.* New York: Corinth.

———. 1871. *Systems of Consanguinity and Affinity of the Human Family.* Washington, DC: Smithsonian Institution.

———. [1877] 1963. *Ancient Society.* New York: World Publishing.

Murdock, George Peter. 1949. *Social Structure.* New York: Macmillan.

Nielsson, G. P. 1985. "States and Nation-Groups: A Global Taxonomy." In *New Nationalisms of the Developed World,* E. A. Tiryakian and R. Rogowski (eds.), pp. 27–56. Boston: Allen and Unwin.

Oboler, Regina Smith. 1986. "For Better or Worse: Anthropologists and Husbands in the Field." In *Self, Sex, and Gender in Cross-Cultural Fieldwork,* Tony Larry Whitehead and Mary Ellen Conaway (eds.). Urbana: University of Illinois Press.

Pasternak, Burton, Carol E. Ember, and Melvin Ember. 1997. *Sex, Gender, and Kinship: A Cross-Cultural Perspective.* Upper Saddle River, NJ: Prentice-hall.

Price, Sally. 1989. *Primitive Art in Civilized Places.* Chicago: University of Chicago Press.

Rabinow, Paul. 1977. *Reflections on Fieldwork in Morocco.* Berkeley: University of California Press.

Rosaldo, Renato. 1989. *Culture and Truth.* Boston: Beacon Press.

Rosenstiel, Annette. 1983. *Red and White: Indian Views of the White Man 1492–1982.* New York: Universe Books.

Sahlins, Marshall. 1985. *Islands of History.* Chicago: University of Chicago Press.

Sanday, Peggy. 1981. *Female Power and Male Dominance: On the Origins of Sexual Inequality.* Cambridge: Cambridge University Press.

Schieffelin, Edward L., and Robert Crittenden. 1991. *Like People You See in a Dream: First Contact in Six Papuan Societies.* Stanford: Stanford University Press.

Schlosser, Eric. 2001. *Fast-Food Nation: The Dark Side of the All-American Meal.* New York: HarperCollins.

Sennett, Richard, and Jonathan Cobb. 1973. *Hidden Injuries of Class.* New York: Vintage.

Serpell, Robert. 1971a. "Discrimination Orientation by Zambian Children." *Journal of Comparative and Physiological Psychology* 75:312–16.

———. 1971b. "Preference for Specific Orientation of Abstract Shapes Among Zambian Children." *Journal of Cross-Cultural Psychology* 2:225–39.

Siskind, Janet. 1973. *To Hunt in the Morning.* New York: Oxford University Press.

Smedley, Audrey. 1993. *Race in North America: Origin and Evolution of a Worldview.* Boulder, CO: Westview.

Spicer, Edward H. (ed.). 1952. *Human Problems in Technological Change: A Casebook.* New York: Sage.

Spradley, James R. [1970] 2000. *You Owe Yourself a Drunk: An Ethnography of Urban Nomads.* Long Grove, IL: Waveland Press.

Stoller, Paul. 1989. *The Taste of Ethnographic Things: The Senses in Anthropology.* Philadelphia: University of Pennsylvania Press.

Tannen, Deborah. 1990. *You Just Don't Understand: Women and Men in Conversation.* New York: Ballantine.

Tax, Sol. 1958. "The Fox Project." *Human Organization* 17: 17–19.

The Globalist. 2001. Globo Quiz: Super-Sizing McDonald's. http://www.theglobalist.com/nor/quiz/2001/07-03-01.shtml (retrieved April 25, 2002).

Thomas, Elizabeth Marshall. 1956. *The Harmless People.* New York: Random House.

Thomsen, Moritz. 1969. *Living Poor: A Peace Corps Chronicle.* New York: Ballantine.

Tonkinson, Robert. 1978. *The Mardudjara Aborigines: Living the Dream in Australia's Desert.* New York: Holt, Rinehart, and Winston.

Turnbull, Colin. 1962. *The Forest People.* Garden City, NJ: Doubleday.

Tylor, Edward. B. [1871] 1958. *Primitive Culture.* New York: Harper Brothers.

———. [1881] 1916. *Anthropology: An Introduction to the Study of Man and Civilization.* New York: Appleton.

———. 1889. "On a Method of Investigating the Development of Institutions; applied to Laws of Marriage and Descent." *Journal of the Royal Anthropological Institute of Great Britain and Ireland* 18:245–72.

Valentine, Charles. 1968. *Culture and Poverty: Critique and Counterproposal.* Chicago: University of Chicago Press.

Van Gennep, A. 1908. *The Rites of Passage.* Monika Vizedom and Gabrielle L. Chaffee (trans.), Introduction by Solon T. Kimbell. Chicago: University of Chicago Press.

Van Willigen. 2002. *Applied Anthropology: An Introduction*, 3d ed. Westport, CT: Bergin & Garvey.

Wallace, Anthony F. C. [1961] 1970. *Culture and Personality,* 2d ed. New York: Random House.

Ward, Martha C. 2005. *Nest in the Wind: Adventures in Anthropology on a Tropical Island,* 2d ed. Long Grove, IL: Waveland Press.

Watson, James L., ed. 1997. *Golden Arches East: McDonald's in East Asia.* Stanford, CA: Stanford University Press.

Weatherford, Jack. 1991. *Native Roots: How the Indians Enriched America.* New York: Crown.

Weber, Max. [1922] 1946. *From Max Weber: Essays in Sociology.* Hans Girth and C. Wright Mills (trans. and eds.). New York: Oxford University Press.

White, Leslie A. 1959. *The Evolution of Culture: The Development of Civilization to the Fall of Rome.* New York: McGraw.

Whiteford, Linda M., and Robert T. Trotter III. 2008. *Ethics for Anthropological Research and Practice.* Long Grove, IL: Waveland Press.

Whitten, Norman E., and Dorothea Whitten. 1988. *From Myth to Creation: Art from Amazonian Ecuador.* Urbana: University of Illinois Press.

Williams, Nancy. 1976. "Australian Aboriginal Art at Yirr Kala: The Introduction and Development of Marketing." In *Ethnic and Tourist Arts: Cultural Expressions from the Fourth World,* Nelson Graburn (ed.), pp. 266–84. Berkeley: University of California Press.

Williams, Thomas R. 1983. *Socialization.* Englewood Cliffs, NJ: Holt-Rinehart.

Williams, Walter. 1986. *The Spirit and the Flesh: Sexual Diversity in American Indian Culture.* Boston: Beacon Press.

Yan, Yunxiang. 1997. "McDonald's in Beijing: The Localization of Americana." In *Golden Arches East: McDonald's in East Asia,* James Watson (ed.), pp. 39–76. Stanford, CA: Stanford University Press.

Zavella, Patricia. 1987. *Women's Work and Chicano Families.* Ithaca, NY: Cornell University Press.

Index